GLASS HANDBOOKS

GLASS AND PRINT

GLASS HANDBOOKS

GLASS AND PRINT

Kevin Petrie

A&C BLACK ▪ London
UNIVERSITY OF PENNSYLVANIA PRESS ▪ Philadelphia

For Sheila Petrie and Allen Doherty for their constant support.
In memory of Terry Petrie.

First published in Great Britain in 2006
A & C Black Publishers Limited
Alderman House
38 Soho Square
London W1D 3HB
www.acblack.com

ISBN-10: 0-7136-6491-6
ISBN-13: 978-07136-6491-1

Published simultaneously in the USA by
University of Pennsylvania Press
3905 Spruce Street
Philadelphia, Pennsylvania 19104-4112

ISBN-13: 978-0-8122-1946-3
ISBN-10: 0-8122-1946-5

Book design by Jo Tapper
Cover design by Sutchinda Rangsi Thompson
Copyedited by Rebecca Harman
Proofread by Julian Beecroft
Project Manager: Susan Kelly
Editorial Assistant: Sophie Page

Printed and bound in China by C&C Offset Printing Co., Ltd.

Frontispiece:
Lark Mirror, Karen LaMonte, USA, 2004. Cast glass with photosensitive sandblasting, 31.5 x 16 x 1.5 cm.

CONTENTS

Glass Balustrade, The Sage, Gateshead, Kate Maestri, UK, 2004.
Screenprinted glass, 200m long. Photo: Philip Vile.

ACKNOWLEDGEMENTS

Writing a book of this nature involves bringing together disparate material from across the world. This could not have been achieved without the kind co-operation of many people and institutions. Therefore, I would like to give my sincere thanks to all of those who have freely offered their time to help me.

I am especially indebted to all the artists, museums, companies and libraries that have sent images and information. In particular, I am grateful to the Museum of Decorative Arts in Prague, the Victoria and Albert Museum in London and the National Archives at Kew, for taking the first colour images of pieces from their collections and allowing me to publish them for the first time. I am also grateful to Johnson Matthey PLC, Tyneside Safety Glass Co. Ltd, Proto Studios, and Franz Mayer of Munich Inc. for providing useful information. The Rakow Research Library at Corning, New York and the Littleton Studios at Spruce Pine, North Carolina, sent invaluable material in the closing stages of the project. A special thanks is due to Ellen E. Fischer of the Littleton Collection for kindly reviewing Chapter 13 and making useful additions. I am also grateful to Clive at sad-mac.co.uk for preparing the images for print. I must also acknowledge and thank Paul Scott whose work on the subject of Ceramics and Print has been an inspiration. Also Helen Maurer and Julian Ewart of the University of the Arts, London, and Professor Steve Hoskins of UWE, Bristol for their advice and assistance.

I must thank the University of Sunderland for supporting this book, in particular through the award of a Research Fellowship, and all my colleagues in the Glass and Ceramics team, especially Peter Davies, Professor Sylva Petrova, Mike Davis and Visiting Professor Dan Klein, for their encouragement, invaluable contacts and advice. In addition, thanks to all the students at Sunderland, on both the BA (Hons) Glass and Ceramics and MA Glass programmes, who have contributed to this book. A special thanks is due to Karin Walland and Andy Conway for their great contribution in Chapters 9, 10 and 11.

I would like to acknowledge the support of the Arts and Humanities Research Board for the award of the grant that enabled the development of 'Integrated Glass Printing'. Also, Northlands Creative Glass, Bullseye Glass Co. and the Royal College of Art supported the further development of the process.

For turning the manuscript into this book, I thank all the team at A&C Black, especially Linda Lambert, with whom I first discussed the idea for a book like this nearly a decade ago, and Managing Editor Susan Kelly for her advice, understanding and humour.

Kevin Petrie, University of Sunderland, 2006

INTRODUCTION

In recent years there has been considerable interest in the creative potential of printing onto alternative surfaces. Particularly apparent in the areas of ceramics and enamels, this has resulted in the development of useful practical information in the form of books, conferences and exhibitions. At the time of writing, little accessible and clear information on the many creative possibilities of glass and print has been produced. This book aims to address this by introducing a range of printmaking techniques that can be used for creative expression across the main areas of glass art: kiln glass, hot glass and architectural glass. This will be of interest to students, designer-makers, artists working on public art commissions and those working on production runs. Throughout, the specific materials, mediums and methods needed for glass and print will be explained.

Printing onto glass offers incredible potential for artists due to the transparency of glass and variety of the printing methods that can be used. For example, in kiln-formed glass printed imagery can be sandwiched within a glass form. Relief surfaces can also be created by casting glass into moulds taken from printing plates. In the area of hot glass (glass-blowing), prints can be applied to glass and blown into three-dimensional shapes to create amazing distortions, or enclosed within the form. In architectural or flat glass a vast range of aesthetic imagery can be directly screenprinted onto sheets of glass in a fast and economic manner.

A personal perspective

My own interest in printmaking for alternative surfaces developed while I was still an undergraduate Illustration student at the University of Westminster in the early 1990s. A visiting lecturer, Ian Morris, told me about transfer printing for ceramics. This was a process little used at that time in the Ceramics Department, and I started to print my illustrations onto ceramics.

Later, this led me to the Ceramics and Glass Department at the Royal College of Art for my MA. Here, I developed an interest in glass, and combined my knowledge of printing with an emerging understanding of kiln-formed glass to produce a group of sculptural head and mask forms with enclosed printed imagery. The printed images represented internal thoughts, memories and feelings.

After graduating from the RCA, I was fortunate to be awarded a studentship to study for a PhD at the Centre for Fine Print Research at the

CASE STUDY: KEVIN PETRIE

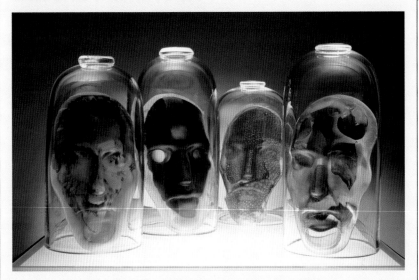

Cell of himself, Kevin Petrie, UK, 1995. Kiln-formed float glass masks with transfer-printed inclusions, free-blown glass bell jars and light box, 45 x 50 x 50 cm. Collection of the Parallel Media Group, London.

This piece was inspired by the line 'And each in the cell of himself is almost convinced of his freedom', from the W.H. Auden poem *In memory of W.B. Yeats* and also Sylvia Plath's book *The Bell Jar*. The glass masks represent our outer selves while the prints show an internal world. The bell jars emphasise that thoughts and feelings are contained inside the envelope of the body. The transfer prints are derived from drawings, applied to flat window glass and fired on. An additional sheet of glass is then fused on top to enclose the print in a separate firing. This is then slumped into a mask-shaped plaster/molochite mould in a third firing.

University of the West of England (UWE), Bristol. This project involved the development of a new, patented, water-based screenprinting system for ceramics, and also brought me into contact with a broad range of printmaking approaches. After this I gained a part-time lecturing post in the Glass and Ceramics Department at the University of Sunderland.

I now lead the Master of Arts in Glass programme at the University of Sunderland and continue research into printing and glass, including the development of 'integrated glass printing' (see Chapter 7), a new process using polymer printing plates and powdered glass, as well as the reestablishing of traditional techniques such as printing from etching plates onto glass (see Chapter 8).

At the University of Sunderland we have set up our own in-house print facility, and I have introduced printmaking for glass to the curriculum. What has really interested me when teaching has been the diversity of approaches that students have taken after I have introduced the basic principles of various processes. In many cases, they go on to develop their own individual variations on glass and print processes in order to express their specific creative ideas. Throughout this book I have used examples of the students' work to show this range of potential. It is worth pointing out that in most cases the works shown are some of the first pieces the students have made using glass and print. I think this indicates that interesting and individual pieces can be made using glass and print after only a relatively short time.

Two artists that joined the MA Glass programme at Sunderland, Karin Walland and Andrew Conway, came with experience in resists and photography respectively, and have kindly shared this knowledge in Chapters 9, 10 and 11. In addition to the student examples, works by international artists also show the exciting creative potential and diversity of approach from what might be called the 'professional end'. A number of case studies give examples of the methods and ideas behind specific pieces of work.

The subject matter of this book falls between two large areas of artistic practice: glassmaking and printmaking. Both have their own distinct history, conventions and technical processes. A book of this size cannot hope to cover all aspects of both subjects; therefore I have confined myself to dealing with issues where the two subjects overlap. If you are unfamiliar with glass or with printing (or with both) you are likely to need to seek guidance from other sources in addition to this book. Where possible I have recommended further reading to help fill in these gaps.

CASE STUDY: JULIAN STOCKS

The Gift (detail – one of three panels), Julian Stocks, UK, 2004. Etched and enamelled glass, 62.5 x 140 x 1 cm. Photographer: Julian Stocks.

This piece by leading architectural glass artist Julian Stocks forms part of an installation of three panels for the Open University. This detail shows a range of print-related processes employed to create a design that exemplifies the education process. The background blue and black are screenprinted, kiln-fired enamels. The white text has been sandblasted through a vinyl mask. The oak leaves are made from flashed glass that has been screenprinted with a resist and then acid-etched to reveal the lighter colour. This is then applied to the larger panel using silicon.

CHAPTER ONE

A HISTORICAL OVERVIEW

Printing onto glass first emerged in the eighteenth century and is now an important strand of both industrial and artistic practice. Over the last 250 years glass and print processes have offered distinctive and pragmatic solutions for the decoration of glass.

Eighteenth-century origins

England is known for the development of transfer-printing onto ceramics in the eighteenth century, and methods for printing onto glass are closely related. Printing onto both ceramics and glass is thought to have first emerged from the manufacture of japan and enamel on copper objects. Japanning is a process whereby objects, usually of sheet iron, are covered in varnish and stoved to produce a hard shiny surface. Japanned ware is commonly black, but can also have clear and coloured surfaces. Decorated trays are a common form for japanned ware. Enamelling on copper involves objects such as snuffboxes being coated in a fine, powdered form of flint glass. After a rapid firing of only a few minutes, a smooth white surface is created. This forms a good base for painted or printed decoration that is fused on in a subsequent firing.

The precise details of the invention of printing onto glass are unclear, and it is likely that several people developed similar processes in parallel. Three petitions for patents made by the Irish engraver John Brooks, between 1751 and 1754, form the basis for the belief that he was one of the main pioneers.[1] Petitions for patents were the first stage in obtaining a patent, and were often filed several months before the patent was granted. Petitions are of especial interest when the application is unsuccessful – as was the case with Brooks – as they are often the only record of an applicant's claim for having developed a new process.[2]

It is thought that Brooks developed a method of printing onto japanned ware around 1751, as in 1752 he was advertising his ability to print japanned trays.[3] He had made his first unsuccessful petition for a patent for printing onto enamel and china the year before. It is thought by some that, as he did not advertise that he could print china and enamels the following year, he had only developed the principles (not the practice) in 1751.[4] This would make sense, as printing onto surfaces such as enamel, china or glass would require ink that could withstand a firing in the kiln to permanently fix

The first page of Brooks's petition for a patent, dated 25 January 1754, perhaps the earliest reference to printing onto glass. Courtesy of the National Archives, ref. SP44/261.

the image. This was not necessary for the japanned ware. As Brooks was an engraver, he was unlikely to have had knowledge of the vitrifiable inks needed at this point.

When Brooks made his first petition he was based in Birmingham. At the time of his second petition on 25 January 1754 he was based in Battersea, London, a centre for the enamel trade, where he became a partner in an enamel works. One theory is that he moved to London in order to develop the process that he had first used on japan ware to include the vitrified surfaces of enamel, china and glass. It is this second petition of 1754 that includes the first reference to printing onto glass:

> Sheweth – That your humble petitioner has found out and discovered the art of printing on Enamel, Glass, China and other Ware History Portraits Landskips Foliages Coats of Arms Cyphers Letters Decorations and other Devices.

Brooks was unsuccessful in all his petitions, and there is some debate about whether or not he actually achieved entirely successful prints on glass. In contrast, there is an alternative argument that his first petition, in 1751, in fact might have been intended to cover glass, as the term 'enamel' was also used in the eighteenth century to refer to white opaque glass as well as enamel on metal.[5]

Whatever the precise details, it is clear that by the latter half of the eighteenth century, glass was being printed on. Evidence for this is available in perhaps the earliest-known piece of printed glass, a flask dated 1760–70 in white opaque glass in the Victoria and Albert Museum, London. The piece is blown, and printed in black on both sides. On one side is there is a horseman in eastern Asian attire hunting a leopard, and on the other a European couple. Here the gentleman, perhaps a gamekeeper, is offering the lady a hare that he appears to have just caught.

Both prints have been coloured with hand-painted enamel. This would have been applied to the fired print and then fired on in a second firing. It is interesting to note that the images do not fit the shape of the flask. This suggests that the prints were made for other shapes, perhaps an enamel snuffbox. This lack of consideration of the combination of form and image is also common in early ceramic printing and gives this piece a rather experimental feel. One might speculate that this is because this is one of the first tests of printing onto glass.

Close inspection of the flask reveals a faint pinkish thumbprint on the surface of the glass. Presumably, the painter had traces of the enamel colour on his or her fingers and passed it onto the flask when holding it during decoration. This trace has then been fired on, fixing the evidence of the artist's hand forever.

It was not until 1781 that the first successful patent for printing onto glass was granted, to Henry Baker, an enameller of Liverpool.[6] In contrast to Brooks's petitions, Baker's patent gives considerable details of both the printing methods and inks used. The basic principle of all early printing for glass, enamels or ceramic involved the transfer-printing of images from engraved or etched copperplates, or sometimes wooden blocks, onto the surface of the ware. First the image would have been cut into the surface of the plate. This forms what is known as an intaglio plate. It would then have been inked up with ink containing an oil-and-enamel pigment. The surface of the plate was then cleaned, leaving the ink in the cut grooves that formed the image. The plate would then have been printed onto a tough, thin tissue paper through a press. This paper, which was rather like the paper used to roll cigarettes, was known as 'potter's tissue', as it was more often used to print ceramics. After printing, the tissue was applied face down to the surface of the ware and the back rubbed to transfer the image. Alternatively, a piece

Flask, 1760–70, English. White glass with printing and hand-painted enamels. This piece is one of the earliest surviving pieces of printed glass. Collection of the Victoria and Albert Museum, London. Photo: V&A Images.

of gelatin or similar, known as a bat, was used instead of the tissue. In some cases clear printing oil would have been transferred to the ware and the powdered colour would have been dusted on. With all these variations, the pieces would have been fired in a kiln after printing to adhere the image permanently.

Nineteenth-century developments

In the nineteenth century there were a number of patents relating to ornamenting glass. In particular, the copperplate transfer method was developed for a range of uses. Advances were made in the application of the print and also in the types of ink used. For example, in 1805 Samuel Anness, a china enameller of London, patented his 'improved methods of preparing enamel colours'.[7] It seems that he developed a palette of colours that could be fired onto glass at lower temperatures than those needed for ceramic, thus avoiding the danger of the glass melting. As he states, 'The object, aim and purpose, in the composition of the said colours, beside their respective tints, consists in making them so fusible as to melt or adhere to vessels of glass by a degree of heat not so considerable as to melt or injure the vessels themselves.'[8] This remains an important consideration today, and you will see in the following chapters that it is important to choose the correct types of colour for the job.

Drinking glass, Bohemia, 1830. Printed in black on a white background. Nineteenth-century examples of printed glass often feature transparent glass with a black print applied to a panel of white enamel. Museum of Decorative Arts in Prague. Photo: Gabriel Urbánek.

In his patent, Anness provided recipes for a range of colours. For example, to make green he says, 'Take one ounce of copper dust, two ounces of sand, one ounce of litharge, half an ounce of nitre, or two of copper, one of sand, two of litharge, one and a half of nitre, mix them with equal parts of flux, or vary the proportions of them as may be found necessary according to the tint of colour required.'[9]

In 1806, John Davenport, a glassmaker in the county of Stafford, patented 'A new method of ornamenting all kinds of glass in imitation of engraving or etching, by means of which borders, ciphers, coats of arms, drawings, and the elaborate designs may be executed in a stile of elegance hitherto unknown, and which cannot possibly be equalled by the usual and customary mode of etching or engraving as hitherto practised'.[10] Although not actually a print technique, this method does have some parallels with printing methods used today. Essentially, Davenport devised a coating for glass that when fired gave a frosted appearance like acid-etched glass. This coating, made of cullet (or broken glass), pearl ashes, red lead and arsenic, could be painted onto the glass and then scratched through to the polished glass below to form a design. When fired, the glass would have a frosted coating with a fine design in clear glass. Today, inks can be bought that emulate acid-etching or sandblasting. These are greyish inks that give a similar effect to abraded glass.

In the mid-nineteenth century the firm of Richardson in Wordsley produced vases with transfer-printed decoration.[11] The themes of the decoration include classical figures based on the Roman Portland vase that had gained much public attention after being smashed at the British Museum in 1845 (it was subsequently repaired). These figures were sometimes printed onto a plain opaline surface or set against a coloured-enamel background. The addition of the coloured enamel would have taken place after the print had been fired onto the glass, to prevent it being damaged.

Acid-etching is another area where the copperplate method had uses. The basic process for etching glass involves the application to the glass of a resist. A design is scratched through the resist to reveal the glass below. The object is then placed in acid, which bites the glass in the exposed areas. Once the resist is removed the design is revealed as a line image. In order to reproduce the design, transfer prints are used to apply the resist to the glass.

The method patented in 1853 by Charles Breese of London[12] was taken up by a number of companies and widely used in the latter half of the nineteenth century. Breese states, 'The invention consists in printing upon paper in an adhesive matter and transferring the impression to the surface to be ornamented. The paper is removed and the pattern has applied to it a powder of some substance which resists the action of acids, after which the surface is exposed to the action of fluoric acid.' This process was used to print bulk orders for souvenirs and articles for hotels, railways and shipping, etc. According to glass historian Charles Hajdamach, this method evolved into the idea of printing an acid paste from an engraved copperplate onto paper and then onto the glass. The paste would bite the design into the glass and was washed off after about two minutes. Again, logos for shipping lines and hotels were decorated using this method.[13]

In the late nineteenth century, printing was used to create resists for sandblasting, which had been invented in the USA in 1870. A resist made of glue, dextrin, glycerine and colouring for body was printed from a copperplate onto tissue and then applied to the glass. In this case the resist protected the glass from the high-pressure jet of sand, stopping it from abrading unwanted areas. Once the resist had been removed the design would be left abraded into the glass.

Twentieth-century developments

The major development in the industrial use of glass and print in the twentieth century was the introduction of screenprinting, in particular, screenprinted transfers. Screenprinting as we known it today was first patented in 1907.[14] The process essentially involves a stencil applied to a mesh screen stretched on a frame. Ink is forced through the mesh by a rubber squeegee (in the areas not blocked by the stencil) onto the substrate to be printed (see Chapter 4 for a more detailed description).

In the 1930s the English company Johnson Matthey developed screenprinted transfers for glass. This method allowed for an image to be printed first onto paper and then applied to the ware at a later date. It was then fired on to form a permanent bond (see Chapter 5). These early screenprinted transfers were initially used to label bottles, and then during the Second World War to print calibrated scales and other markings for

Novelty glass ball with paper prints, filled with plaster, early twentieth century, Tyne and Wear Museums.

scientific, surgical and other instruments.[15] This transfer-printing method was later developed into the prime method for decorating industrial ceramics: the 'water-slide' transfer.

It was in the 1970s and 1980s that screenprinting for the decoration of glass really became significant. This was largely due to advances in screenprinting that allowed for finer and more sophisticated imagery to be printed. Other methods, such as direct printing and heat-release transfers, were also developed. The latter involved a wax layer on the transfer that when heated allowed for the automated application of transfers. This provided the advantage of faster production times, as the previous, water-slide method had had to be applied by hand.

Current industrial applications

Today, the glass-printing industry produces printed glass for a surprising range of applications. Screenprinted decoration allows for a broad range of

CASE STUDY: TYNESIDE SAFETY GLASS CO. LTD

Tyneside Safety Glass Co. Ltd, UK screenprints the black 'obscuration bands' onto the windows for buses and tractors.

1 (Right) After the glass has been cut to shape, the flat sheets are placed on the bed of a semi-automatic screenprinting press.

2 The bed then moves under the screen, and the glass is automatically printed.

3 The glass is removed using suction grips, so as not to mark the printed black border, and placed in the dryer, seen on the right.

4 The flat sheets are then placed in a bending furnace that both curves the glass and fires the black printed enamel. This takes about one hour.

5 During a laminating process, the printed glass is bonded to a second, plain layer using both heat and pressure. The finished windows are then ready to be shipped to vehicle manufacturers.

effects and imagery to be applied to glass: for example, advertising and logos on tumblers, beer glasses, and perfume bottles. Advances in computer technology allow for the rapid design and production of decoration in full colour for different market demands.

Items such as hi-fi stands, decorative mirrors, shower doors and cooker hobs and doors commonly feature printed glass. In architecture, a gradated dot matrix is often printed onto glass for what is termed in the industry 'Solar Control' and 'Privacy Control'. Contemporary fashion for clean, uncluttered interiors has led to the development of all-over glass cladding for bathrooms, replacing the need for separate tiles and grouting. These glass panels are screenprinted on the back to give the required colour. The glass in telephone boxes is screenprinted with logos in either coloured inks or 'etch' ink, a pale-grey ink that when fired gives the appearance of etched or sandblasted glass. These designs are printed because the logos are often too complex to sandblast in the high volumes required.

In the automotive industry, advances in glass adhesives mean that windows for cars, buses, tractors and trains are now usually glued into position. The join around the edges of the window is screenprinted with an 'obscuration band' in 'automotive black' both to protect the UV-sensitive polyurethane glues and to disguise the join. Direct screenprinting is the most economic and rapid process for this high-volume sector. In the same field, the rear-window heating system in cars is screenprinted onto the glass with heat-conducting inks. The 'No Smoking' signs on London Underground trains are also screenprinted onto the windows.

Photography and glass

Although the focus of this book is printing onto glass and not photography on glass, which has different principles, it is perhaps useful to briefly describe some of the developments in the combination of glass and photography.

Shortly after the invention of photography in the first half of the nineteenth century, sheets of glass started to be used to make negatives. According to Martin Harrison, a writer on art, photography and stained glass, the first experiments with applying positive photographs to glass began with the transferring of collodion images by the French scientist and photographer M. Samson in 1854.[16] Collodion is a thick, colourless solution of pyroxylin, ether and alcohol used to make photographic plates. In 1860, a process was patented by F. Joubert that involved images fired onto glass that had been coated with albumen, honey and ammonium bichromate. Photographic images fixed onto glass plates, often in decorative lead work, became especially popular in France, and in the 1880s the Ceramic Stained Glass and Vitrified Photograph Company briefly exploited the potential of glass and photography in England.

In the 1930s and 1940s the laboratories of the US company Corning Glass Works developed 'photosensitive glass'. This research was initiated by a

The Relationship of
Time Within Time,
Mary Van Cline, USA,
2000. Photosensitive
glass, jade *pâte-de-
verre* glass, cast black
glass, 61 x 79 x 15 cm.

Corning scientist, R.H. Dalton, who noted the phenomenon that certain
transparent, copper-containing silicate glasses develop a red coloration when
they are reheated after cooling, especially when exposed to ultraviolet light.[17]
This was later developed into a range of photosensitive glasses by S.D.
Stookey and W.H. Armistead. The glass looked like conventional glass, but
contained tiny metallic particles that were mixed into the glass during
manufacture. The glass had to be kept out of the light until use, as it was
light-sensitive. To create the photographic image, a negative was placed
against the glass and exposed to ultraviolet light. The glass was then heated
and the photographic image appeared. The image was not only on the
surface, but could extend into the glass for up to 2 inches. At the time,
various colours were possible depending on the type of glass. Both clear and
opal glasses were also made.[18] The new glass was said to have application for
portrait and scenic photographs, photographic murals, decorative windows,
advertising displays, church windows, etc. At the time of writing this glass
appears to be out of production.

In 1978, the US artist Mary Van Cline began using a photographic liquid
emulsion to produce photographs on glass. In the following year, she worked
with Kodak in Rochester, New York, and with their help began to use a
custom-designed, ortho-based emulsion that they coated on glass using an
industrial vacuum process. Cline went on to order these plates a year in
advance in quantity until 2003, when Kodak disassembled their entire glass-
plate division to make room for digital processes. She is now working with
Dupont Industries to fabricate large glass photos that are up to 2 by 3 metres.
Van Cline combines the photographic image on glass with cast-glass
elements to create complex symbolic sculptural works.

Form – Animal Faces, Per B. Sundberg, Sweden, 2000. Irregular blown hollow form in clear glass, with printed images of dogs, cats and horses inside the glass; the interior is lined with opaque glass. Approximately 25 cm high. From the *Fabula* series for the Orrefors factory. Collection of the Victoria and Albert Museum, London. Photo: V&A Images.

The use of glass and print by artists

Developments in printed glass up until the 1980s appear to have been largely industry-led. Since then artists have adopted and developed the methods for their own creative ends, sometimes in collaboration with industry. In the UK 2003 Jerwood Applied Arts Prize for Glass, three of the six shortlisted artists – namely Helen Maurer (winner), Amber Hiscott and Alexander Beleschenko – used screenprinting in their work. This shows that as well as having significance in the industry, printing is now an important method in the artist's canon of techniques for applying imagery to glass.

Glass and print is especially prominent in contemporary architectural glass. There is also a range of interesting work emerging in the areas of hot glass and kiln glass. This is perhaps largely confined to art schools, where consistency and economic factors are less pressing than in the industrial or public-art sector. There is great potential for development in these areas, and as interest develops in the creative potential of print for alternative surfaces it is likely that more exponents will emerge. The recent purchase by the Victoria and Albert Museum of a piece by Per B. Sundberg with printed transfers and hot glass is an interesting example of this development.

CASE STUDY: AMBER HISCOTT AND DAVID PEARL

Water towers, Phase 1, Callaghan Square, Cardiff, Wales, (night-time view and detail), 2000. Height 10 metres.

This piece consists of 32 panels of toughened and laminated float glass mounted on a structure of stainless steel posts. This shows that direct printing is not only confined to flat glass. The flat glass was printed first with opaque enamels and then curved in a kiln. The twin towers, representing earth and fire, are positioned in the centre of a pool and herald the approach to Cardiff Bay.

The importance of print in architectural glass

Architectural glass is perhaps the area where printing onto glass has been most highly developed by artists. Today, large sheets of float glass can be toughened for safety. Modern fixture systems mean that many sheets of glass can be combined and integrated into architectural spaces to form screens, canopies and internal and external walls. Technology even allows for whole façades to be made from glass.

This glass can be decorated with a range of methods including hand-painting, rollering, airbrushing, acid-etching and sandblasting, which have practical as well as artistic purposes, such as privacy and controlling the transmission of light. Printing, and in particular screenprinting enamels, is also a useful tool in these situations, as it offers the potential for diverse,

CASE STUDY: SASHA WARD

Two windows, Tadley Pool, Hampshire, Sasha Ward, UK. Screenprinted enamels fired onto glass.

UK architectural glass artist Sasha Ward has been working with enamels fired onto glass for about 18 years. She started using enamels to try and achieve several transparent colours on one piece of glass. When the commissions she undertook became larger, she found that the only way to get a strong transparent colour over a large area was to screenprint the enamel. She now works with a factory (Proto Studios) for large commissions, and also screenprints, hand-paints and sandblasts smaller works in her own studio.

CASE STUDY: CATRIN JONES

Vaulted window, Central Provisions Market, Newport, South Wales, 2003. Screenprinted enamels on float glass, 120 m². Made by Proto Studios Ltd. Photographer: Tim Pegler.

This window was commissioned for the redevelopment of a Victorian indoor market. The image shows a broad scheme of flowers, leaves and the family, and represents the interaction between the market's commercial produce and its traders and customers.

CASE STUDY: MARK BAMBROUGH

As well as being used to create new works of art in architecture, printing onto glass is also being developed as a tool to conserve traditional stained glass. These windows often require physical and environmental protection in the form of secondary glazing. This can take many forms, from plastic sheeting to mirror-image leaded panels, in which the main lead lines of the stained glass window are replicated. While all current systems of secondary glazing have a functional justification, they also generate glare and reflection, which can seriously interfere with both the interior and exterior aesthetics of the building in which they are sited.

The purpose of the research undertaken by conservator Mark Bambrough was, therefore, to produce a highly functional but aesthetically more acceptable form of protective glazing. This was achieved by screenprinting, with ceramic enamels, a photographic image of the exterior appearance of the stained glass onto a flat pane of glass. This copy was then kiln-formed using a full-sized mould to match the contour lines of the existing leadwork pattern. The research produced a three-dimensional glass facsimile that reflected back all the life and colour that existed in the original stained glass. The facsimile is also as transparent in transmitted light as the industry-standard mirror image described above, and opaque in reflected light; there-fore the image is seen from the outside yet burns out on the inside. Its advantage over conventional methods of protection is that, as it responds to surface light in a similar way to that of the stained glass it is protecting, and

does not give off glare or reflection, it is unobtrusive. It also functions aesthetically with the building, by breaking up and diffusing light play, while retaining the relationship between glass and stone that existed before the secondary glazing was introduced.

Window (c1890s) by Stephan Adam with protective screenprinted glazing by Mark Bambrough (exterior view), Newkilpatrick Church, Bearsden, Glasgow.

Swimmers, Brian Clarke, UK, 1974. Leaded glass with screenprinting. An early example of the combination of printing and architectural glass, made by Clarke as a trial panel at the age of 21 for the 'Preston Guild window' of St Mary's church, Preston, Lancashire. © Brian Clarke.

multicoloured, large-scale imagery that is durable as well as decorative.

These developments have revolutionised the field of architectural glass. Some artists talk of their printed glass works as being a modern form of stained glass. However, contemporary applications for printed glass are now not confined to churches and cathedrals, as might stereotypically be thought of traditional stained glass. Religious buildings do still offer a context for creative glass, but secular spaces are becoming increasingly common for art. Hospitals, leisure centres, retail outlets, corporate buildings, rail stations and airports are all examples of architectural spaces where glass is used functionally and decoratively to provide added layers of meaning.

Experiments with print by architectural glass artists are known from the 1960s, for example, Mike Davis's use of lino-printed silver stain in 1969 (see p.70). Later, in 1974, the eminent architectural artist Brian Clarke produced perhaps one of the earliest screenprinted photographs on glass in the UK, for St Mary's Church, Preston, Lancashire. However, it is not until the 1980s and increasingly in the 1990s that there is evidence of the use of glass and print really developing on a significant scale in the architectural glass sector. During this time artists started to work with fabricators to produce printed glass works on a larger scale. Today the prime companies include Proto Studios in the UK, Franz Mayer of Munich Inc. in Germany and Derix Glass Studios also in Germany.

Printing from glass onto paper (vitreography)

This book is largely concerned with printing imagery onto glass. However, glass has also been used as a substrate from which imagery can be printed off, rather like an etching or lithography plate. This was first attempted in the 1840s in Vienna. Using the fumes of acid, sheets of glass were etched and the subsequent prints were exhibited at the Crystal Palace in London.[19]

The key developer of printing from glass in the twentieth century was American artist Harvey K. Littleton, who is often described as the 'father of American studio glass' as he was the first to set up a glass-blowing course in an American university, in 1962. Techniques for producing vitreographs include both intaglio and planographic methods (see Chapter 13).

Littleton made his first prints from glass in 1974 after a workshop on sandblasting techniques. He asked a friend to print some sheets of glass that had designs sandblasted into them. The results were promising, and by the late 1970s Littleton had devoted a part of his glass-blowing studio to printing from glass. He also started to invite friends to try and develop the process, for example, Erwin Eisch from Frauenau in Germany. Eisch is from a family of glasscutters and engravers, and brought this expertise to abrading and cutting the surface of the glass plates.

Trial II, Harvey Littleton, USA, 1975. Vitreograph; three colour relief print from a glass plate hand printed on Arches acid free paper, 45 x 60 cm. This is one of the early examples of printing from a glass plate. In this case hot glue was drawn onto the glass to act as a resist before sandblasting and then printing. Courtesy of Littleton Studios.

Later, the term 'vitreography' was coined to describe the developing repertoire of new printing techniques from glass.[20] Through the 1980s and 1990s Littleton continued to develop vitreography with a number of master printers at his North Carolina studio. This has resulted in several hundred editions of prints with a great diversity of imagery by a number of painters and printmakers as well as artists from the glass world, including Dale Chihuly and Stanislav Libensky (see pp.115 and 117).

The twenty-first century

Recent years have seen the development of digital prints from converted computer printers, direct digital printing, and also the emergence of laser-printed wet-release decals (Lazertran). Both methods offer the advantage of speed and convenience, but remain limited, compared with screenprinting, in terms of the scale that is possible and, in the case of Lazertran, in terms of durability. Having said that, these methods are likely to evolve rapidly and in time may replace the current standard methods. For now, though, traditional print methods used in conjunction with glass remain an area with great potential for creative exploration, especially in the artist's studio.

Notes

[1] Documents held by the National Archives, Kew, UK. The first petition is in SP44 – 260, p. 513 and the second and third in SP44 – 261, pp. 55 and 85.

[2] See Watney, B. and Charleston, R.J., 'Petitions for Patents concerning Porcelain, Glass and Enamels with special reference to Birmingham, "The Great Toyshop of Europe"', *English Ceramic Circle*, 1966, Vol. 6, No. 2, pp. 57–123.

[3] This is mentioned by Cyril Williams-Wood in *English Transfer Printed Pottery and Porcelain* (London, Faber and Faber, 1981), London, where he refers to Benton, E., 'John Brooks in Birmingham', E.C.C. Transactions, Vol. 6, Part 3, 1970, p.162.

[4] Ibid. p.54.

[5] See Charleston, R.J., *Decoration of Glass – Part 4, The Glass Circle* (1972) for more detail on early printing on glass. Also Charleston, R.J., 'English Opaque-White Glass', *Circle of Glass Collectors*, Paper No. 111, pp. 1 ff.

[6] Baker's Specification: Ornamenting Glass.,Patent No. 1296, 1781.

[7] Anness's Specification: Enamels for Ornamenting Glass, Patent No. 2900, 1805.

[8] Ibid., p.2.

[9] Ibid., pp.2–3. Litharge is lead monoxide, and nitre is potassium nitrate.

[10] Davenport's Specification: Ornamenting Glass, Patent No. 2946, 1806.

[11] Charles Hajdamach describes many of these and other developments in his book, *British Glass 1800–1914*, Antique Collectors Club, 1991.

[12] Breese, Charles. A method of forming designs and patterns upon papier-mâché, japanned iron, glass, metal and other surfaces. Patent No. 1714, 1853.

[13] Charles Hajdamach, *British Glass 1800–1914*, Antique Collectors Club, 1991., p.198.

[14] Simon, S. Improvements in or relating to stencils. Patent No. 756, 1907.

[15] See Freeman, P., 'Lithographic and Screenprinted Transfers', *Ceramic Industries Journal*, No. 92, December 1983, pp.24–7.

[16] See Harrison, M., *Combining mediums – Brian Clarke and Linda McCartney*, Brian Clarke and Linda McCartney – Collaborations, Musée Suisse du Vitrail, Romont, 1997.

[17] See Garbowski, B.J., *Photosensitive Glass – Trail of Research*, Rakow Research Library, Corning Glass Works, 1978, or Blakeslee A.L., 'Printing Photos inside Glass', *Popular Science*, November 1947, for useful overviews of developments in this area.

[18] For a more detailed account of the chemistry involved in photosensitive glasses see, Stookey, S.D., 'Photosensitive Glass – A new photographic medium', reprinted from *Industrial and Engineering Chemistry*, Vol. 41, p. 856, April 1949.

[19] Kessler, J., *Luminous Impressions – Prints from Glass Plates*, Mint Museum, North Carolina, 1987, p.11.

[20] For a useful overview see, Byrd, J.F., 'Littreography', *Glass: The Urban Glass Quarterly*, No. 72, Fall 1998, pp. 12–25.

CHAPTER TWO

MATERIALS FOR GLASS AND PRINT

Many of the processes described in this book are very similar to methods of printing onto paper. However, there are important differences in the printing mediums and colourants used. There are also several types of glass that might be used for printing.

Inks for printing onto glass

Ink consists of a colourant, often in the form of powdered pigment, and a medium. The medium, which can be solvent-based or water-miscible, acts as a carrier for the colour during printing. Most of the methods described in this book involve the fixing of the colourant onto the glass with heat to form a permanent or semi-durable bond. This heat is usually achieved by placing the printed glass into a kiln.

The need for heat to fix the print requires a special type of colourant. Standard inks for printing onto paper would burn away in the kiln. Therefore, a vitrifiable colourant must be used. This means that while the printing medium burns away, the colourant remains and is changed into a glass-like material through the action of heat.

For printing permanent images onto glass, the colourant used in most cases will be an 'enamel'. Enamels are comparatively low-firing glass frits containing metallic oxides as the colouring agent; these are available in powder or paste form. The methods given in this book mostly use powdered enamels. They can be mixed with appropriate mediums and used for printing, painting and spraying glass.

Enamels are available in either opaque or transparent form. This relates to the appearance after firing. It is possible to add a transparent flux to opaque enamels to increase transparency. They also come in different firing temperatures. This can cause some confusion, because the lower-firing enamels tend to be used for glass (approximately 550-650°C/1022-1202°F) and the higher-firing for ceramic (approximately 750–850°C/1382-1562°F). This is because, unlike ceramic, glass objects will melt at the higher temperature. Therefore, the lower-firing range are described as 'glass enamels' and the higher-firing range as 'ceramic enamels'. However, in some areas of the 'glass world',

A range of enamel powders in the unfired state. Courtesy: Johnson Matthey PLC.

the term 'ceramic enamels' is sometimes used to describe all enamels. This is important to bear in mind when choosing and buying enamels. It would be advisable to check that the firing temperature is suitable for your aims.

Other colourants can also be used for printing glass, such as stained-glass paints, 'Paradise paints', silver stain (silver compounds that produce colours from pale yellow to deep brown) and lustre.

Printing mediums

The printing medium that you choose will largely depend on your method of printing, i.e. direct screenprinting, screenprinted transfer, etching, linocut, etc. Perhaps one of the main issues will be whether to use a solvent-based or water-based (more accurately water-miscible) medium. In basic terms you will need to use a solvent-based medium if you are making transfers, as the print will have to survive submersion in water. For direct printing onto glass, a water-based medium will be suitable. For printing from a metal etching plate onto glass you can use standard copperplate oil used to make etching ink. The suppliers of enamels and mediums will advise on the products suitable for your requirements.

The table below gives a general guide to the sorts of printing materials that you might require for different types of glass printing. More detail is given in the relevant chapters and in the directory at the end of this book (p.122).

Type of glass printing	Colourant	Suitable printing medium	Where do you get them?
Direct screenprinting onto flat glass	Glass enamel, glass paints, silver stain. Etching paste can also be used for a frosted effect	Water-miscible screenprinting medium, clove oil-based universal medium. Glass paints may need to be thinned	Ceramic and Glass suppliers
Screenprinted transfers (decals)	Glass or ceramic enamels, ceramic underglazes or oxides. Use ceramic enamels if you intend to subject the piece to temperatures over 650°C, for example, by re-forming blown pieces or by additional kiln-forming	Solvent-based screenprint medium for transfers	Ceramic and Glass suppliers
Printing from an etching plate onto glass	Glass or ceramic enamels, depending on the temperature you need to go to	Medium copper plate oil, Potters tissue to transfer the image	Copper plate oils are available from printmaking suppliers
Lino-printing and relief	Glass enamel, glass paints, silver stain	Clove oil, clove oil-based universal medium	Stained-glass suppliers, ceramic and glass supplier. Lino is available from general art and printmaking suppliers
Sandblast resists	None needed	None needed – you use the film as a resist for sandblasting	See Directory
Acid-etching resists	None needed – see Directory (page 122) for acid-etching pastes	None needed – you use the film as a resist for acid paste. You can also screenprint bitumen, circuit resists, Brunswick black or Rhinds turps-based stop-out varnish to act as an acid resist	See general printmaking suppliers for stop-out varnish. Bitumen (or roofing tar in the USA) is available from hardware stores
Photography (traditionally bichromated gelatin with the addition of ferric oxide)	None needed	Use a photographic emulsion	Photography suppliers
Digital prints and films	None needed, supplied by manufacturer	None needed for digital prints. Lazertran paper needed for wet-release transfers	See Directory
Cold colours	A number of standard inks can be applied to glass that do not need to be fired on. These have varying degrees of durability	Colours are likely to be supplied ready to print	Printmaking inks suppliers

A selection of the printing materials required for different types of glass printing.

Types of glass

Float glass

Float glass is available in flat sheets of various sizes and thicknesses, and is perhaps the most commonly used glass for printing at present. Sometimes known as 'window glass', float glass was developed in the UK by Pilkington's of St Helens. It is produced by floating a continuous ribbon of hot glass out onto a bath of molten tin. This results in a 'tin side' with a slight iridescence, and a non-tin side. The non-tin side is usually the one that is printed on.

This type of glass is usually used in architectural contexts where safety and strength are paramount. Float glass can be strengthened to create toughened or tempered glass. The process involves the heating and rapid cooling of the glass to create high compression. This creates a bending strength that is four to five times higher than normal. It also means that, if broken, the glass will shatter into many small harmless pieces.

After printing, float glass can be fused together in the kiln to sandwich the print. It can also be slumped into moulds to form new shapes.

Antique glass

This is a term used to describe sheets of glass produced by the cylinder method and mainly used in leaded stained-glass work. A long bottle shape is blown to form a cylinder known as a 'muff'. This is split lengthways and flattened in a kiln. This creates glass sheets, available in many colours, of slightly uneven thickness and surface. Some artists prefer this more 'characteristic' aesthetic to the very predictable appearance of float glass. Antique glass can be printed in the same way as float glass.

Flashed glass

This is a subset of antique glass. Flashed glass is glass with a thin layer of another colour of glass added to one side. This can be printed with a bitumen resist and the surface layer removed with acid to reveal the colour below (see chapter 10). The same can be achieved with sandblasting by using Fablon™ (or other sticky-backed plastic) as a resist (see Chapter 9).

Blowing glass (furnace glass)

This glass is available as pellets or cullet and is melted in a furnace for use in glass-blowing. The most common method for printing onto blown glass objects is transfer printing. Transfers can be applied to glass objects such as vases and glasses and fired on. They can also be applied, fired on and then reheated and blown out to create a distorted image. Alternatively, the printed object can be encased in a second layer of glass so that the printed image is inside the glass (see Chapter 5).

Casting glass

Casting glass is available from specialist suppliers in many colours in blocks (ingots) or as cullet. This glass is melted in the kiln in a mould to create the desired form. Printed transfers can be applied to ingots of glass and cast. The printed images will then be encased within the glass form and will often appear to 'swim' as they distort with the movement of the glass as it melts (see Chapter 5).

Firing and annealing

Annealing is the process during firing, or, in the case of blown pieces, after manufacture, in which the stresses in the glass caused by heating and cooling are reduced by holding the glass at its annealing temperature for an appropriate period. The annealing temperature and the annealing time relate

CASE STUDY: DAVID PEARL

Interior screen for the Princess of Wales Hospital, Bridgend, Wales, David Pearl, UK, 1999. Enamels screenprinted onto 13.5 mm bent and laminated glass, 7 x 2.1 metres.

Architectural glass artist David Pearl developed the original artwork for this piece using paper stencils torn from a life study of a reclining figure, reflecting the patient's condition and the history of the figure as an object of beauty. This piece shows an effective use of the combination of opaque and transparent enamels.

to the nature of the glass, its thickness, its coefficient of expansion, and the surface area exposed. If annealing is not carried out, the glass may break during firing or even some years later. Before firing a print onto glass you should first check with the manufacturer for an appropriate annealing cycle.

It is also important to note that different types of glass should not be combined together in hot processes unless you are sure that they are compatible, as otherwise they may break at some point. Again, suppliers will advise on this.

Health and Safety

When using any materials or processes in art and design one must take note of health and safety guidelines. The Control of Substances Hazardous to Health regulations (COSHH) and risk assessments are now a major consideration in any studio. The area of glass and print presents some potential hazards for the unsuspecting artist. For example, many of the printing mediums used may require the wearing of a mask to prevent inhalation of the fumes. This is especially the case with solvent-based products, where you should also ensure adequate ventilation. Gloves should also be worn where necessary to prevent skin contact. You should also wear a mask or respirator when handling enamels, mould-making materials, fine glass frits and any other dust-like materials. Great care must be taken when handling glass to avoid the risk of being cut. When using heat to form glass you should follow guidelines given in the studio that you are working in. If setting up your own studio, you will have the legal responsibility for your personal safety and that of workers and visitors. Avoid eating or drinking in glass or ceramic studios and ensure that materials are cleaned up after use. Acid presents a particular hazard and its use is not covered in detail in this book. Specialist guidance should be sought before you use any material that you are not familiar with. Most products will have Health and Safety Data Information Sheets (or MSDS Reports in the USA), which must be adhered to. In most cases common sense is perhaps the best safeguard.

CHAPTER THREE

PREPARING ARTWORK

As screenprinting is perhaps the most popular method used to print onto glass, this chapter concentrates on how to prepare artwork for screenprinting. It includes simple 'low tech' methods as well as processes that require the reproduction of an image or design using what can loosely be termed 'photographic' means to form a stencil. These principles can then be applied to other processes discussed later in the book.

Preparing artwork for a screenprint

If you are unfamiliar with screenprinting and its uses you may first want to read Chapters 4 and 5. You might also consider reading a book on screenprinting for paper, for example, *Water-based Screenprinting* by Steve Hoskins. This will give important insights into screenprinting in general. You can then use this book for the specifics relating to glass.

Before you can make a screenprint you need to prepare the artwork for the image that you want to print. This artwork is known as the 'positive', and will take one of two forms: autographic or photographic. Autographic relates to artwork that is drawn by hand and includes that which is painted, drawn or cut by hand. Photographic is artwork that is created solely by photography or on the computer. This will often take the form of a photocopy, scan or computer-generated image.

Autographic stencils

Simple stencils
A paper stencil is perhaps one of the simplest methods of masking areas of the screen mesh to create an image. This method is useful if resources are limited and only a few prints need to be made – perhaps up to ten. It does not require the use of a photosensitive emulsion. The image is first drawn or traced onto a piece of paper (greaseproof paper works well). You then cut away all the areas that you wish to print with a sharp knife, tack the stencil onto the bottom of the screen with some masking tape or blobs of printing ink to hold it in position, and print. If you are only printing a few pieces of glass it is also possible to use sticky-back plastic and stick that directly onto

CASE STUDY: PAUL SCOTT

Paul Scott's book *Ceramics and Print* was a catalyst in the phenomenal growth of printmaking within studio ceramics. In recent years he has begun exploratory work, transferring ceramic printmaking materials and technologies to glass. Most of the processes and many of the materials detailed in *Ceramics and Print* can, with creative adaptations, be used on glass.

Test glass tile by Paul Scott, made with photocopy decal sandwiched between two sheets of float glass (5cm x 7cm)

An example is the use of photocopies offering a 'low tech' alternative to screenprinting. Certain models of laser printers and photocopiers contain iron oxide[1].

The easiest way to transfer a laser or photocopied image is to print onto conventional transfer paper[2]. The resulting image is turned into a transfer by simply applying a thin layer of covercoat with a credit card or squeegee. Once dry this is used like a conventional transfer. The image can also be transferred without covercoat. The glass is made sticky with spray mount adhesive. The un-lacquered decal is placed face down onto the sticky glass surface and rubbed to make good contact with the adhesive. Sponging the back of the transfer allows it to be slid off leaving the print stuck to the surface of the glass. As the fired colour is simply iron oxide it needs to be fired to a high enough temperature so that it is fused to the surface, or sandwiched between layers of glass (over-firing can cause the image to fade).

Cumbrian Blue(s) bowl, printed ceramic underglaze decal by Paul Scott in blown glass form by Robert Geyer, 20 cm x 12 cm, made Red Deer College Canada, 2004. Unfired decal sheet alongside bowl.

[1] Not all machines carry iron in their toners, and you will need to experiment to find out if you have access to a suitable copier or laser-printer. The simplest test is to simply burn a piece of copied/printed paper. If the resulting ash has brown residues it is very likely that iron is present.

[2] Never use U-WET or Lasertran in mono lasercopiers or mono photocopiers as the fusing temperatures in these machines is in excess of the melting point of the covercoat on these papers. Serious damage to expensive hardware could be the outcome of careless experimentation with these papers.

CASE STUDY: TERESA ALMEIDA

1 **2**

3 **4**

Using a sticky-back plastic stencil, Teresa Almeida (Portugal). Note the last image shows an example of a different printed colour.

MA student Teresa Almeida covered sheets of glass with sticky-back plastic (Fablon) and then cuts a design out of it with a sharp knife. She printed the colour through an open screen and carefully removed the plastic before firing.

the glass as a mask. This should be removed before firing. Masking fluid, a rubber-like liquid often used in watercolour painting, can also be painted onto the glass to form a resist. This should be carefully removed before firing.

Knife-cut films

If you wish to print simple, solid shapes, a knife-cut film such as Amberlith™ or Rubylith™ is useful. This is used in conjunction with a direct photographic screen emulsion to block out light in the areas that you want to print. These films consist of an orange or red plastic coating on a transparent polyester backing sheet. The design is cut through the coloured layer with a very sharp knife. The backing sheet should not be pierced. Unwanted areas of coloured film are then peeled away to leave the design that you want to print in orange or red still attached to the backing sheet. This is then used as the positive when exposing the screen emulsion to ultraviolet light. This technique can be used in other print methods that involve exposure to ultraviolet light.

You can also use knife-cut films that are applied directly to the screen to form a stencil. These are designed for use with solvent-based inks.

Drawing films

There are a variety of translucent films available that can be used to draw and paint on to create screenprintable artwork. The advantage of producing

The use of textured film to create hand-drawn marks, and how they print.

Textured drafting-film original

Graphite stick

Dio pen using
Staedtler ink

Ink with
methylated spirit

Ink with sandpaper
scratches

Chinagraph pencil

Chinagraph pencil

Gouache with knife
scratches

Ink with Vaseline
(petroleum jelly)
resist

Screenprinted result

your artwork on a film, rather than working directly on the screen, is the greater variety of aesthetic effects you can produce with a wide range of drawing and painting materials. For simple shapes or bold designs, drafting films such as Kodatrace or Permatrace are very effective. These have a shiny side and a matt side. You should draw on the matt side. Due to their very smooth surface these films are best for imagery that is flat as opposed to textured, for example, precise line work in ink. Rotring film ink and Photopaque (available from screenprint suppliers) are especially effective for drafting films.

For a more textural image you should use a film with a textured surface such as Mark Resist or True-Grain (or 'Lexan' in the USA) . Because of the textured surface, these films give a textural structure to the drawing. A broad range of drawing and painting materials and methods can be applied to these films, creating an almost infinite range of aesthetic effects. This versatility offers great potential for producing screenprintable artwork for glass. It can also be used for print processes using ultraviolet light.

You can also use tracing paper or tissue to produce artwork, although as they are more delicate than drafting films care should be taken when drawing on them. They are also less effective than textured films for producing textured artworks.

Photographic stencils

Almost any kind of image can be printed using a photographic stencil, including photographs, text, solids, fine lines and computer-generated artwork. If you want to reproduce a photograph you should remember that screenprinting and the other print methods in this book cannot print true tone. When the ink passes through the screen onto the paper or glass below, it remains the same tone throughout the image. In order to create the illusion of tone, an image must first be broken down into dots in what is known as a halftone. A newspaper photograph is an obvious example of this. In a black and white halftone image the image is made up of different sizes of black dots that interact with the white paper to produce the effect of a tonal range from black to white.

A coloured halftone image is made up of four colours: cyan, magenta, yellow and keyline (black). This is known as a CMYK image. Here the dots of all the colours interact to create the illusion of many more colours. CMYK printing can be used in direct printing, but this is very difficult as all the colours need to fit together very accurately. It is much easier to print CMYK images onto paper and then transfer them to glass.

The simplest forms of photographic positives are photocopies or laser prints. Paper photocopies or laser prints can be made translucent by coating them with liquid paraffin or vegetable oil. Alternatively, you can produce a photocopy on acetate. It is important to remember, with all types of positive, that the image should be as opaque as possible to achieve the best results. Sometimes a photocopy on acetate can be somewhat weak. Using two photocopies on acetate at the same time during exposure can help counter this tendency. Naturally, you will have to take care to line them up accurately to avoid a blurred image.

For a less crude image you can use a laser-copy film such as Laser Film Matt or Clear by Folex Imaging. This is a polyester film that can pass through a laser printer or photocopier without heat distortion. It is a cheap and effective method for producing basic designs such as text or simple halftone images.

A photographic stencil does not have to reproduce a photographic image. They can also be used to reproduce drawings. For example, you might wish to reproduce a drawing from a sketchbook. Rather than redrawing this onto a film like True-Grain it could be photocopied or scanned and printed out onto Folex. The advantage of this is that you can manipulate the drawing before printing it. For example, you might want to change its size or make some corrections. This can be done on the computer or photocopier prior to printing out.

Computer-generated artwork

This is perhaps the most common method of developing photographic artwork for screenprinting. As well as scanning photographs and drawings to output onto film for screenprinting, you can also scan actual objects. The important thing to remember when scanning is to decide if you are scanning black and white or colour. If you want to produce a CMYK image you will need to select RGB colour before scanning. You will also need to select the resolution of the image. This relates to the fineness of the picture. For screenprinting, a resolution of 150 dpi (dots per inch) should be sufficient unless you intend to increase the printed image to a much larger version than the original that you are going to scan.

If you wish to manipulate the image, then the Adobe PhotoShop program will be useful. This is used by most publishers and designers to develop and modify images. It can be used to combine elements into one image, to make corrections, change dimensions, etc. In fact, you can achieve virtually any affect. For further details on computer-generated artwork see *Digital Printmaking* by George Whale and Naren Barfield.

CMYK four-colour images

If you want to produce a full-colour image you will need to scan the image and break it down into CMYK. You can do this in PhotoShop by saving your completed image as a CMYK-mode image. After this, follow the steps below to output as separations:

- Go to 'Page Set-up' under the 'File' menu.
- Select 'Screen'.
- Deselect 'Use Printer Default Screens'.
- Under 'Frequency' specify the lines-per-inch output. This is your halftone screen resolution (for a 120 screen an average would be 47 lpi). Under 'Angle' type '67°'. Under 'Shape' select 'Ellipse'.
- Select 'Magenta'.
- Under 'Frequency' specify the lines-per-inch output (47 lpi). Under 'Angle' for magenta type '37°'. Under 'Shape' select 'Ellipse'.
- Select 'Yellow'.
- Under 'Frequency' specify the lines-per-inch output (47 lpi). Under 'Angle' for yellow type '97°'. Under 'Shape' select 'Ellipse'.
- Select 'Black'.
- Under 'Frequency' specify the lines-per-inch output (47 lpi). Under 'Angle' for black type '7°'. Under 'Shape' select 'Ellipse'.
- Click 'OK'.
- Select 'Registration Marks'. These are marks to help alignment when setting up for printing.
- Select 'Calibration Bars'.
- Select 'Labels'. This labels each positive so you know which relates to each colour.

You can then print these colour separations onto Folex, or if you need very high-quality images you can get them printed onto film at a commercial reprographics bureau. These bureaux produce high-quality film artwork for printers from computer disks. They will be listed in the telephone book under 'Typesetters' or 'Printers' Services'. You should ask for 'right-reading film positives, emulsion side up'.

The screenprinting of CMYK images requires some considerable expertise and is not covered in this book. Therefore, you should seek advice from an experienced screenprinter before attempting it yourself, or else consult a book on screenprinting. You can buy sets of CMYK enamels, but this can be very expensive, as the magenta enamel contains gold. If you only want to produce a few prints you might do better to get a company to produce the transfers for you, or use the digital system described in Chapter 12.

CHAPTER FOUR

DIRECT SCREENPRINTING

Screenprinting is perhaps the most common method of printing onto glass.
It allows for the production of a broad range of imagery, from a very loose,
hand-drawn style to photographic images and text. It is particularly useful
for printing flat sheets of glass.

Overview of screenprinting

There are two prime ways screenprinted imagery is applied to glass: direct
printing and transfers. Direct screenprinting involves printing imagery
straight onto glass, whereas transfer prints are printed onto paper then
transferred to the glass via a plastic-like 'covercoat' layer. Transfer printing,
described in the next chapter, is commonly used to apply imagery to three-
dimensional objects and for fine-detail designs.

Direct screenprinting is usually applied to flat sheets of glass. Artists using
screenprinting on glass are likely either to produce small-scale work in their
own studio or an open-access print studio, or large-scale work using a
specialist fabricator.

Screenprinting involves the use of a wooden or metal frame with a mesh
stretched over it. Traditionally, the mesh was made of silk, as opposed to the
polyester used today, hence the term sometimes used for this process,
'silkscreen'. It is also worth mentioning that other terms have been used to
describe screenprinting, including serigraphy and mitography.

In the making of a screenprint, a design is applied to the screen in the
form of a stencil that blocks areas of the mesh. Therefore, during printing
the ink can only pass through the mesh in the places that remain unblocked.
Stencils can take a number of forms, and are applied either directly or
indirectly. An indirect stencil might be a sheet of paper with a design cut out
of it. A direct stencil is a photosensitive emulsion that actually coats the
screen and impregnates the mesh. Once dry the coated screen is exposed to
ultraviolet light through a 'positive' of the image. The positive is in fact a
positive (as opposed to a negative) opaque image of the design that you want
to print on some form of translucent substrate. This is usually a paper or a
plastic-like film (see Chapter 3).

During exposure to ultraviolet, the light passes through the translucent
material of the positive substrate and causes the areas of photosensitive
emulsion on the screen that are exposed to the light to harden. Where the

CASE STUDY: BOB BUDD

Split Sky, Bob Budd, UK, 2003. Screenprinted photograph of an image of the sky, sandwiched between toughened float glass and held by stainless-steel framing, 105 x 78 x 2 cm. Photographer: Bob Budd.

Budd prints photographic imagery onto glass. Printing and firing enamels produces permanent images that have the luminosity he wants. He says that it might be feasible to use Cibachrome – if the images did not need too long a life – or to put a photo emulsion onto the glass, but these methods present problems of longevity, as the image could be scratched off. Therefore, in this case screenprinting is the most practical method to achieve both the permanence and the required look.

light is blocked by the opaque image on the positive, the emulsion remains unaffected and can be washed out of the screen with a spray of water. This also fixes the remaining emulsion on the screen. You are then left with the screen mesh blocked, except in the areas that correspond to those represented by your opaque design on the positive. These unblocked areas will allow ink to pass through during printing.

To print the image, a squeegee, a long square-edged piece of rubber attached to a handle, is used to pull a pool of ink across the screen. This forces the ink through the mesh in the places where the stencil is not blocked and onto the paper or, as described in this chapter, flat piece of glass. If a suitable form of ink has been used on the glass, the resulting image can then be fired on in a kiln to fix it permanently.

CASE STUDY: JOANNA HEDLEY

Hedley, an MA student, makes drawings from life reflecting important events and places in her life. In this work she uses the theme of love and marriage. The printed image in black is derived from a section of a drawing photocopied onto acetate to make the positive and then screenprinted onto flashed glass. After firing the print onto one side, Hedley has then used glue as a resist on the other side and sandblasted through the pink layer of glass to reveal the clear layer underneath.

Wedding day, Joanna Hedley, UK, 2003. Glass panel comprised of screenprinted enamels on pink flashed glass, 30 x 30 cm.

It should be noted that screenprinting is a very broad subject, on which many excellent books have been written. This chapter can only give an overview of the process and highlight the special considerations that need to be taken into account when screenprinting onto glass. Therefore, if you are new to screenprinting, it would be advisable to read around the subject and perhaps seek some extra guidance. There are many regional night classes and print studios that offer introductions to screenprinting onto paper. You can then use this book when moving to glass. Even just watching someone else make a screenprint can be invaluable. It is often only when the whole process has been seen that the reason for all the stages becomes apparent. Also, when you are new to the process it can seem rather complex. However, once you are familiar with the technique, it is in fact very quick. This is especially the case if you need to make more than one print of the same image.

Screens

Today, screens are relatively cheap to buy. Therefore, it is not necessary actually to make your own frame and stretch the mesh over it. However, if you are especially keen to do this you will find instructions in some early screenprinting manuals, such as *The Thames and Hudson Manual of Screen Printing* by Tim Mara or *Screen Printing Techniques* by Sylvie Turner.

A ready-made screen can be made of wood or aluminium. Wood has a tendency to warp in time, so aluminium is perhaps better if you can afford it. An important aspect to consider when choosing a screen is the mesh size. In most cases this is denoted by a number and a letter, for example, 120t (USA: 305t). The number refers to the number of mesh threads per centimetre and the letter relates to the diameter of the mesh thread. The letter 't' denotes a standard diameter. For water-based inks you would normally use a 120t (USA: 305t) for autographic stencils and a 150t for photographic. For solvent-based inks a 90t (USA: 230t) is more common for autographic stencils and 120t for photographic. A finer mesh, perhaps 120t, would be used for transfers. A coarser mesh, perhaps 90t or below, might be used for direct printing. The coarser the mesh, the thicker the depoit of ink.

Making a screen stencil

Once you have prepared your artwork as a positive you can then prepare your screen stencil. You first have to choose a screen that is an appropriate size for your artwork. If you place your artwork in the middle of the screen there must be at least a 13 cm gap between the edge of the image and the inside of the screen frame. This is to allow room for the ink and squeegee during printing. You can, of course, place several images on the screen as long as this 13 cm border is maintained. Do not be tempted to skimp on this, as you may encounter problems later during printing. It is better to use more than one screen rather than try to fit too many images onto one.

Coating the screen

To make a photographic stencil on your screen you must first coat it with a light-sensitive emulsion. This is a light-sensitive polymer that is available in several forms. The easiest and most versatile for most users are diazo-based, such as Folex Dc200 or Kiwicol Poly plus W. Ulano supply the US equivalents. These consist of two parts that must be mixed together: an emulsion and a sensitiser. Once mixed they will last in the fridge for up to four months, or eight weeks at room temperature. The lid must be kept firmly in place as much as possible due to light sensitivity. The emulsion is applied to the screen mesh by means of a coating trough. It is vital that the trough is completely clean and has no nicks or dints along its lip, as this will create a mark in the stencil. The trough is usually made of metal, with plastic ends that are attached to contain the emulsion. A generous amount of emulsion is poured into the trough to a depth of 2 or 3 cm (1 in.). Insufficient emulsion in the trough can cause incomplete coverage of the screen.

For coating, a clean and dry screen should be lodged against a secure surface, for example, a lath of wood attached at a slight angle to a wall. The coating trough is then offered up to the bottom of the screen. Once in contact with the screen it should be tilted so that the emulsion slowly runs forward and makes contact with the mesh. As soon as all the front of the emulsion is touching the screen mesh the trough is drawn up the screen, leaving the mesh evenly coated. When you reach the top of the screen you should tilt the trough back slightly to allow the emulsion to draw back from the mesh, and then move it away. This prevents blobs of emulsion falling down onto the screen when the trough is removed. Avoid coating in direct sunlight and do not take more than a few minutes for each coating.

You then quickly remove the screen to a dark area to dry. This can be a specially designed drying cabinet or a dark cupboard or room. The screen should be heat-dried at around 35-40°C/95-104°F. If you do not have access to a drying cabinet, a fan heater will do. Do not expose the screen until the emulsion is completely dry.

It is important to return the emulsion in the trough to the pot. A good way is to hold the trough vertically over the pot, remove one of the plastic ends and then scrape the emulsion down into the pot with a plastic palette knife, a rubber kidney as used in ceramics, or a piece of card. Having returned the excess emulsion to the pot, you should thoroughly clean the trough with warm soapy water. Do not forget to wash the plastic ends as well.

Exposure

Ultraviolet light sources come in two main types: those with a separate light source and print-down frame, and those with an integrated light source. In the first type, the screen and positive are placed on a glass surface with a rubber vacuum sheet placed on top. This secures the positive and screen during exposure. In the second type, the light source is contained within a box with a glass panel on top. The screen and positive are placed on the glass and again secured by a rubber vacuum sheet. A lever is pulled that opens doors in front of the light source, thus exposing the screen.

To expose the screen, place your positive right side up (your image should be the way round that you want it to print) onto the clean glass of the exposure unit or print-down frame . Place the screen onto the glass with the mesh in contact with the positive. Make sure when positioning the screen

CASE STUDY: HELEN MAURER

Ultra Light Frame, Helen Maurer, UK, 2001. Installation shot and detail of glass model, projected image size variable, approximately 3 m². Photographer: Neil Reddy.

Maurer creates subtle reflections on the ideal and reality of memory. A glass model is placed on an overhead projector. Light passes through the objects to create a 'life-size' projected image of the scene on the wall. The model scene has been disrupted: the chair and windbreak have blown over. The toys have been left, yet the projected image reads as an 'ideal', ordered view. The piece creates a dialogue that reflects on the discrepancy between reality and memory. This piece is partly based on family holidays spent caravanning in the New Forest. The aeroplane represents where Maurer thought everyone else was going. Screenprinted enamels onto a piece of glass create the shadow of the trees in the projected image.

that there is at least 13 cm between the edges of the image on the positive and the screen frame. The positive and the screen mesh must be in complete contact with each other during exposure. To achieve this the exposure unit or print-down frame will have a rubber vacuum sheet. Pull this down and turn on the vacuum. This sucks out the air and creates a tight contact. If you have a more simple type of exposure unit you may have to create this contact with a rubber or foam sheet, a board and some weights. Just the board and weights will be adequate for artwork that is not too fine, but you will need to be careful not to damage the mesh.

The exposure times will depend on the type of unit, the age of the light source and its distance from the artwork. If you are working in an established screenprint studio – for example, in a college or open access facility – the staff are likely to be able to advise on exposure times. Failing this, you will have carry out some tests based on the manufacturer's instructions to ascertain the exposure time that gives the sharpest image on the screen that also will not break down during printing.

Once the screen has been exposed, you should remove it from the exposure

1 Pouring light-sensitive emulsion into the coating trough.

2 Coating the screen.

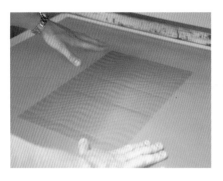

3 Positioning the positive and screen on the print-down frame.

4 Ultraviolet light source and separate print-down frame with screen and positive ready for exposure.

5 Washing out the stencil. Note that the yellow areas are the open parts of the mesh that will allow ink through, while the green areas are the hardened emulsion blocking the screen.

unit immediately and wash out the stencil. To do this you can use a tap fitted with a spray head. For small screens this can be done in the sink or bath at home. In a print studio there is likely to be a specific sink designed for the purpose. You should use a gentle spray and wet both sides of the screen (back first), making sure that you spray all over the emulsion area. This will wash out the areas that have not been exposed to the ultraviolet light and will leave them open so that ink can pass through. Take care to wash away all the surplus emulsion, as a residue can cause water-based inks to harden. You should now let the screen dry out thoroughly before printing. Some printers advise that the screen should be exposed again after washing out for a minute or so to thoroughly harden the emulsion. This will largely depend on the type of set-up you have used. Again, the print-studio staff will advise on this.

CASE STUDY: BRIAN CLARKE

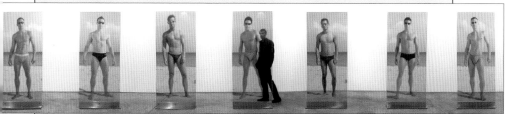

Clarke is perhaps best known for his large-scale architectural projects. However, this suite of seven panels formed part of a solo exhibition, Transillumination, at the Tony Shafrazi Gallery in New York. Although an autonomous piece not reliant on an architectural context, the work still makes references to architecture. The classical beauty of the figures is forever fixed, through both the origin of the image (photography) and the fired print on glass. Consequently, these monumental pieces make one reflect on mortality and the passing of time.

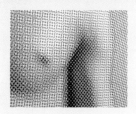

Studies for *Caryatids*, Brian Clarke, UK, 2002. Float glass screenprinted in three colours, each panel 208 x 91 cm. Photo: Roberto Portillo.

The detail shows how the image is broken down into a dot structure that from a distance reads as a coherent photographic image. The panels are composed of three laminated layers with a separate enamel colour on each, creating a sense of space. The blue and yellow are transparent colours and the black is opaque, allowing for some areas to be seen through while other parts, such as the sunglasses, remain impenetrable.

Preparing the screen for printing

Your screen is nearly ready to print now, but first you must spot out any small pinholes of open mesh that you do not wish to print. Small bits of dust will often block the light during exposure and leave these pinholes in the screen. These can easily be seen if you hold the screen up to the light. Use a water-based filler (such as Safeguard Water Soluble Green Filler made by Gibbon Marler) available from screenprint suppliers. This should be mixed 50:50 with water and applied with a small brush. Spotting out is only really necessary if you have a very precise image that would be spoiled by unintended spots of ink.

Having spotted out the screen and let the filler dry, you now need to tape up areas of the screen not covered by the emulsion. This also helps when cleaning ink off the screen, as the tape stops ink getting trapped in the corners.

Setting up for direct-printing flat glass

When printing a flat sheet of glass, a simple set-up comprising a wooden screen hinged to a board is useful. Failing that, for single prints or where registration is not vital, you can just position the screen over the glass and print. You may have to get someone to hold the screen in place. A few small pieces of card should be taped onto the corners of the screen to lift it above the surface of the glass (about 4 mm should be sufficient). You could also use a standard vacuum hand bench, but the use of the vacuum is unlikely to be necessary. This section assumes that you will use the simple hinged screen set-up as shown in the illustrations.

First attach the screen to the hinged baseboard. The glass should be clean before printing and any sharp edges that are likely to come into contact with the screen must be linished off (the glass supplier might be able to do this) or covered with masking tape. Then position the glass under the screen so that

1 A basic screenprinting set-up with hinged baseboard and attached screen.

2 The positive (in this case a photocopy from acetate) taped to a sheet of glass to enable correct positioning. Note the three pieces of card to 'register' the glass.

CASE STUDY: TOM PEARMAN

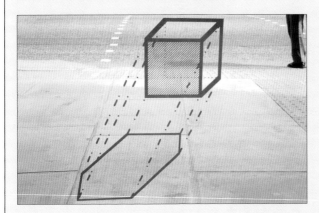

Architectural glass panel, Tom Pearman, UK, 2000. Screenprinted enamels fired onto glass, 140 x 65 cm. One of 16 architectural glass panels for the 30-metre long gallery window of the London Print Workshop.

Pearman, a graduate in Printmaking from the Royal College of Art, was commissioned to create a representation of the history of graphic communication to complement the modern style of the building. Having previously worked with Super Gloss inks on glass, which are durable but not colour-fast, it was necessary to use fired enamels for this piece, which required a permanent lightfast solution. The images can be viewed from both inside and outside the gallery. As can be seen in this image, the view from inside creates an illusionary interplay with the exterior view.

the image will print in the correct place. You can stick the positive onto the glass in the correct position and then line it up with the stencil by looking through the screen. Remember to remove the positive before printing. Once the glass is in the correct position you should mark its location by placing three strips of card flush against the edges as shown in the illustration. This is especially important when you intend to print more than one colour, as you will need to register the glass each time you change the colour to ensure that it is printed in the correct place.

It is now important to set the 'snap'. This is the distance between the screen mesh and the surface of the glass. The mesh should not be touching the glass, as this will cause a blurred image when you print. In order to lift the screen to create the snap distance, you should either tape some pieces of card to the front corners of the screen or onto the baseboard. The snap should be around 4 mm for a tight screen, and you can feel this by gently pressing the surface of the mesh onto the glass below. If the screen mesh is slack, use a greater snap distance.

It is advisable to print a test onto paper before printing onto the glass. This

CASE STUDY: MARK ANGUS

The background red glass is printed with black-glass enamels. The technique used was to tear strips of newsprint and to paint these with the enamel and then place them onto the glass surface, lifting them off straight away. In the lower section there is a verse from a hymn, printed in glass enamel, fired onto white opal glass. The text was copied onto an acetate and screenprinted onto the glass to create the effect of a hymn-book page. Angus describes the angels as 'art historicisation, taking an image from the past and reusing it'. He wanted a group of figures – a choir – and remembered a Van Eyck painting that he had seen in Bruges 28 years earlier. He found that he had a postcard

showing a detail of the group of women. This was enlarged up to A2 size, reduced to only either black or white, then copied onto an acetate and screenprinted. He repeated and reversed the image a few times to make up the number of singers he needed. Angus experimented with this image on different glass types, and with different paint and technique combinations. He made a number of test pieces, eventually settling upon float glass (window glass) and black enamel. The print was slightly overfired. This distorted the glass a little and gave an aged appearance. Silver stain (silver nitrate) was used for the yellow areas to lift the image and give it richness.

Choir window, Eardisley Church, near Hereford, Mark Angus, UK/Germany, 1994. Printed glass, mouth-blown glass and lead, 300 x 250 cm.

allows you to check that the image is as you want it and the ink is thick enough. In screenprinting, the first print is usually lighter than the rest, so printing the paper first means that your glass print will be stronger. To do this you will need to remove the glass and place a sheet of scrap paper underneath the screen. Your registration marks will allow you to return the glass to the correct position afterwards.

CASE STUDY: DAVINA KIRKPATRICK

Kirkpatrick mainly works on commissioned glass projects for architectural contexts. In contrast, this piece forms part of a series of gallery-based works exploring her origins. The pieces contain suggestions of landscapes, journeys and childhood memories. The screenprinting in this piece shows her fascination with maps – two-dimensional representations of three-dimensional space.

Roots II, Davina Kirkpatrick, UK, 1998. Wall piece comprised of direct-screenprinted glass and copper with additional hand-painting with transparent enamel.

Mixing the ink

Once the screen is in position you should prepare your ink. Some inks may be supplied ready-mixed, in which case you can use them straight away. However, if you are using powdered enamels you will need to mix them with a printing medium. For direct printing, a special water-based or solvent-based medium is used (suppliers will advise on this). This should be mixed with the enamel powder of your choice. Remember to consider what firing temperature you intend to use, as this will influence the choice of enamel. If you are simply going to fire the image onto the glass, a lower-firing glass enamel can be used. However, if you want to print the glass and then kiln-form it, perhaps fusing another sheet on top or slumping the glass into a mould, you should use a higher-firing ceramic enamel. This is because kiln-forming the glass requires temperatures of around 800°C (1472°F), which may result in a glass enamel fading. You might also use non-firing inks. These will not be as durable or as lightfast but will be adequate for some interior uses.

The manufacturers of specific printing enamels will supply information on recommended mixing ratios for enamel and medium. You should add the enamel powder to the medium and thoroughly stir it. The consistency of the ink should be quite thick, perhaps like yogurt. If you are only printing one small piece of glass there is no need to mix a large quantity of ink: enough for a generous line about 1 inch wide corresponding to the length of the squeegee will be adequate. Use a plastic spatula to mix the ink, as this can then be used to clean the screen after printing. Metal implements should not be used on the screen mesh, as they can split the screen.

In industry the ink is usually mixed through a triple roll mill to create a homogenous mix. For the small-scale user, a glass muller and a sheet of sandblasted glass can be used to mix the ink. A pestle and mortar is another quick option.

As with all materials you should follow the manufacturer's health and safety guidelines. With enamels you should wear a mask to avoid breathing in the powder and should be careful not to leave enamel on work surfaces where others might pick it up on their hands and ingest it.

Printing flat glass

To print, pour a pool of ink along the front of the screen. Take the squeegee and push the ink forward to the top of the screen whilst holding the screen off the area to be printed so that the paper is not printed. This is called 'flooding the screen' and is important because it deposits an even coating of ink into the mesh and helps prevent the ink drying in the screen between prints. Having flooded the screen, put it down and place the squeegee blade behind the line of ink at the top of the screen. Hold the squeegee at an angle of about 60° and pull forward. This will push the ink through the mesh and onto the paper below. Lift the screen and flood to prevent the ink from drying in the screen. Quickly remove and check the print. If you are satisfied with the image, place the glass under the screen in the registration marks and print. Be careful not to push down too hard where the squeegee comes into contact with the end of the glass, as this could damage the screen or move the glass. If you are printing more than one sheet of glass, remove the printed piece to somewhere safe, place another in registration and continue, remembering to flood after each print stroke.

When you have finished printing, place some scrap paper underneath the screen, gather as much ink as possible and pull it with the squeegee to the front of the screen. You can then lift most of the ink up off the screen and onto the squeegee. Return the ink to the pot and cover it. Then clean the screen with water or solvent, depending on what ink you have used.

Cleaning off the stencil

When you have finished with a stencil it should be removed with an appropriate decoating chemical. Diluted household bleach can be used with

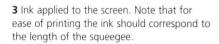

3 Ink applied to the screen. Note that for ease of printing the ink should correspond to the length of the squeegee.

4 Push the squeegee to flood the screen. Note that the screen must be lifted slightly to avoid printing. The card in the bottom right corner creates the 'snap'.

5 Pull the squeegee forward to print.

6 The image printed onto glass. Allow to dry before firing. It could then be hand-coloured with enamels.

7 After printing remove excess ink.

8 Wash with a sponge and water if using a water-based medium. Solvent-based mediums need to be cleaned with an appropriate cleaning agent. A cloth or paper towel can be used once the majority of ink is removed. Rubbing the top and bottom of the screen at the same time with two cloths is effective for a final clean.

DIRECT SCREENPRINTING

CASE STUDY: ROBERT PRATT MCMACHAN

Rosa Sub Rosa (left) and *Moth Light* (right), Robert Pratt McMachan, UK, 2004. Screenprinted enamels on glass, frame, fabric, 90 x 65 x 21 cm and 59 x 37 x 36 cm.

These hanging glass lights consist of three or more layers of glass (plus one of fabric). The glass is screenprinted with alternating opaque and transparent fired glass enamel. The phrase 'Sub Rosa' means 'under the rose'. This comes from a tradition, adopted by the Romans, of denoting something secret with the symbol of the rose. These works can be viewed either lit or unlit; therefore, the 'secret' is the colour and the moths attracted to the light, which can only be viewed when the prints are backlit.

Using a high-pressure hose to remove the stencil.

care, but a specially produced decoating chemical is probably the safest and most effective option. The supplier of the emulsion that you use will be able to advise you of the most appropriate decoating agent.

Place the screen in a washing trough and spray with water on both sides. Spray on the decoating chemical and leave for two minutes. Gently wash away excess emulsion and chemical, and then blast with a high-pressure hose to remove any stubborn areas. If the stencil is hard to remove you could re-apply the decoating chemical and leave for longer. Once clean, the screen should be

CASE STUDY: JULIAN STOCKS

These two windows for the Wellcome Trust building at the University of Dundee take the theme of DNA research as the theme. The images of the stopwatch and the eye, shown in the detail, were selected by scientists at the university through a workshop programme. These were distorted anamorphically to represent the often conflicting points of view at the heart of scientific debate. The detail shows a piece of blue flashed glass that has been screenprinted with a Brunswick black resist, then acid etched, to reveal the lighter colour below. To create the anamorphics, images were scanned into a computer, distorted using PhotoShop and then direct-screenprinted in enamels that were fired on.

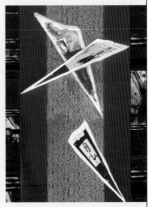

Uses of Disorder, Julian Stocks, UK, 1998. Glass decorated with screenprinted enamels, sandblasting and acid-etching, 1300 x 120 x2 cm. Photographer: Steve Bennington.

thoroughly dried before recoating. It can be dried in a special drying cabinet or placed in front of a fan heater. Be careful not to overheat the screen, as it may split the mesh. Screens can also be left at room temperature to dry. If you have used a solvent-based ink, you will need to degrease the screen after removing the stencil. Screenprinting suppliers will advise on the appropriate products for this, although vinegar can be used as a basic degreaser.

CHAPTER FIVE

SCREENPRINTED TRANSFERS

Screenprinted transfers, also known as decals, enable the production of fine artwork, such as photographs, and the decoration of three-dimensional objects. They also allow for imagery to be enclosed within kiln-formed and blown glass.

Uses of transfers

Although transfer-printing processes were first invented in the UK in the mid-eighteenth century, the standard transfer process of today was developed by the firm Johnson Matthey in the 1950s. This is known as the 'water-slide' transfer or decal. As the name suggests, transfer printing enables the conveying of an image from one surface to another. 'Decal' is an alternative term for the transfer, derived from the French word *décalquer* meaning to trace or copy. In simple terms transfer printing involves printed imagery being transferred from paper to objects such as glass and ceramics.

The advantage of using a transfer, as opposed to direct printing, is that finer and more tightly registered imagery can be printed onto paper and then applied to the ware. This is because it is much easier to print fine imagery onto paper than onto a piece of glass. In addition, unlike an image printed directly, the covercoat transfer is capable of decorating complex multi-curvature objects due to the flexible nature of the covercoat. In industry, cylindrical vessels can be direct-screenprinted mechanically. This involves the object, perhaps a tumbler, moving underneath the screen in a circular motion. However, for the small-scale artist wanting to print similar objects, the transfer method is likely to be the most practical. Another advantage of transfers is their long shelf life of up to five years once printed, allowing a design to be stored and used when needed without having to warehouse decorated stock.

To produce standard transfers, enamels are mixed into an appropriate solvent-based medium and screenprinted onto a gum-coated transfer paper. Over this, a thermoplastic layer called 'covercoat' (or 'overprint' laquer) is screenprinted, slightly overlapping the image area. When thoroughly dry the transfer is soaked in water. This dissolves the gum layer and releases the covercoat and adjoined image from the backing paper. Transfers are applied to the glass face up, and smoothed down with a cloth or rubber kidney. The residual gum from the transfer paper helps to adhere the transfer to the glass surface as well as lubricating the transfer during positioning. During the

CASE STUDY: CATHRINE MASKE

Libelle 2, Cathrine Maske, Norway, 2004. Free-blown white glass with a clear gather over the top incorporating screenprinted transfers, 11 x 23 cm. Photo: NoHokusPokus.

Maske, one of Norway's leading designers has explored the use of screenprints of photographic imagery in glass for a number of years. In the *Libelle* series the inspiration comes from collections of endangered insect species at the Museum of Natural History in Oslo. Maske photographed some of the dragonflies and transferred them to the glass – creating a permanent container for them. The shape of the object is deliberately simple to intensify the lens-like effect, the feeling of looking through a microscope at the preserved creatures. The insects are beautiful and fascinating, but at the same time frightening and strange.

firing, the covercoat layer burns away cleanly, as does the printing medium, leaving the enamel image bonded permanently onto the glass.

Making transfers

There are two types of transfer. Which one you use will depend what the transfer will be used for. The standard transfer is the water-slide or covercoat transfer outlined above. It is also possible to buy pre-covercoated transfer paper. With this product, the image is printed onto a layer of covercoat, thus eliminating the need to print it yourself. This has the advantage of saving on time and effort. However, the disadvantage of this method is that the layer of covercoat on the precoated paper is much less flexible and more brittle than the covercoat that you can print yourself. Therefore, it is harder to decorate more complex forms that have curves in several directions, such as spheres. Cylindrical shapes present much less of a problem.

It should be noted that the covercoat layers on the two types of paper are, in fact, composed of different ingredients. Therefore, you should not attempt to print on top of standard covercoat, as the image is likely to be disrupted during firing. To make transfers, you will need to prepare the artwork and screens as described in Chapters 3 and 4.

Printing transfers

One of the main differences between direct printing and printing transfers is the printing medium used. For direct printing a water-based medium can be used. When printing transfers, a solvent-based medium needs to be used, as the transfer has to be soaked in water and so must be waterproof. Although a water-based transfer system has been developed for ceramics, this process is not suitable as yet for use with glass enamels.

When using solvent-based mediums it is important to find a studio with the appropriate extraction facilities. If you are working in an educational establishment or open-access print studio, the technical staff will advise on this. If suitable extraction is not available it is possible to print basic transfers outside using a hinged screen attached to a baseboard.

Printing onto paper is very similar to printing directly onto glass. The ink should be mixed in a similar manner and to the same consistency as in direct printing. Remember that if the ink looks thin on the paper after you have printed it, it will still look thin once you have fired it onto the glass. If this is the case you might want to clean the screen, add more enamel to the ink and start again. This will save you time in the long run.

You must remember to carefully register the paper before printing so that you can position it again during covercoating. It is important that, once you start printing, you keep going as quickly as possible to prevent the ink drying in the screen. You will need to flood the screen between printings, as described in Chapter 4. After printing, the screen should be cleaned with a solvent. The manufacturer of the medium will recommend the appropriate cleaning agent.

Once the prints are dry you can covercoat them. To do this you must first make another screen stencil that will completely cover your image with about a 5 mm overlap. You can make the artwork for this by painting black ink or Photopaque onto drafting film or True-Grain, or cutting the shape out of card. This is then used to make a screen stencil as described in Chapter 4. If you only have to covercoat a few prints you can roll the covercoat on thinly with a small sponge roller. This is a rather crude method, and it is advisable to print the covercoat for longer runs.

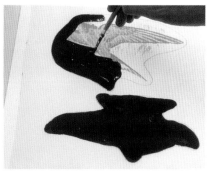

1 Non-covercoated prints of birds by MA student Richard Wheater (UK). The artwork for these images was made by photocopying images from a book onto acetate (you should check the copyright when doing this). Wheater has printed the blue, waited for the ink to dry and then overprinted the same image but in a different position and in black to create a sense of movement.

2 Making the artwork for the covercoat stencil. A piece of True-Grain has been laid over the dry print to be covercoated. Opaque black ink is then painted onto the True-Grain to completely cover the printed image and give a border all the way round. This is then exposed onto a screen as described in Chapter 4.

3 The stencil for the covercoat, ready to be printed. Note that the print image has been positioned underneath to ensure that all of it will be covercoated. Its position has been marked underneath with masking tape so that all the prints can be covercoated in the right place.

Applying transfers to glass

First you will need to wet the transfer. This can be done by placing it under the tap and wetting the back, or by dipping it into a bowl of water. Leave the transfer for a few minutes. If you are going to apply several transfers, they can all be wetted at once and left on a plate. Do not leave the transfer floating in a bowl of water, as the residue of the gum layer will be washed away and the transfer may not stick to the surface of the glass so well. After a few minutes you should be able to hold the transfer between your thumb and forefinger and gently move the covercoat and image layer away from the backing paper. Do not completely remove the backing paper until you are ready to apply the transfer, as it is very flimsy and will be difficult to handle.

CASE STUDY: MARKKU SALO

A graduate of the Department of Industrial Design at the University of Industrial Arts, Helsinki, Salo combines the design of production utility ware with a more experimental approach in sculptural exhibition pieces. The ancient buildings of the Middle East inspired this piece.

Colossus, Markku Salo, Finland, 1989. Mould-blown greyish-blue opal glass, cast-glass base and lid, transfer prints, 58 x 15 x 15 cm.

Make sure that the object to be decorated is perfectly clean. Methylated spirits (solvent alcohol) can be good for this. Wet the surface of the object and then place the transfer, image side up, in the position that you want it. Gently slide the backing paper out from underneath the covercoat/image layer. You can then position the transfer correctly. Wetting the surface of the glass prior to applying the transfer allows the transfer to slide around. Once it is in the correct position the excess water underneath the transfer should be wiped away. This can be done by gently smoothing down the transfer with a rubber kidney. Working from the centre outwards make sure that the transfer is in full contact with the surface of the glass and that all air bubbles are removed. Any remaining moisture can be wiped off with a paper towel. The object should be left to dry thoroughly before firing.

Cut out the transfer. After contact with water you can slide the transfer from the backing sheet onto the object.

Remove air bubbles and excess water with a rubber kidney, then remove any last traces of moisture with a paper towel.

CASE STUDY: KATHRYN WIGHTMAN

BA student Wightman first made a coloured vessel, or 'embryo', in hot glass. When this was cool the screenprinted transfers, of black texture, were applied and fired on in a top-loading kiln. When still hot, the embryo was picked up with a blowing iron and gathered over with a clear layer of glass. White powder was then applied, covering the form. Once cool a stencil was applied and the piece sandblasted to reveal the figure with printed texture and the coloured layer beneath. This was then picked up for the third time and gathered over with a layer of clear glass and blown to the final shape. Corkboards were used to flatten the piece. The figures on the pieces represent individual personality traits. From left to right, Plain Jane, Sexy Bitch and the Mother figure. As Wightman says, 'Wouldn't it be nice if when you wake up in the morning you could decide who you wanted to be today?'

Who do you want to be today? Kathryn Wightman, UK, 2004. Free-blown glass incorporating screenprinted images, approximately 40 x 20 cm.

Applying transfers to blown glass

Transfers can be applied directly to pieces of blown glass and fired on. In this case you will need to use glass enamels for the print. The piece can also be reheated and reworked after the application of transfers. Ceramic enamels are best for this as they can better withstand the high temperatures involved. You will first need a blown-glass blank, or embryo, made of clear or coloured glass. It could also be a cased piece (this means that two different colours are combined in layers: one colour forms a skin or 'case' around the other). Apply the transfer in the usual way and then fire on in a kiln. Pick up the blank on the blowing iron while it is still hot, and form it into the desired shape. Another layer of clear glass can be used to cover the piece and enclose the print.

Applying transfers to kiln-formed glass

'Kiln glass' is a term used to describe the shaping or fusing of glass in a kiln. This most often involves the use of a plaster and molochite (1 pint water, 1lb plaster, 1lb molochite) mould into which the glass will melt with the action of the kiln's heat. This book cannot cover the large range of kiln glass methods. For those wishing to find out more on kiln glass, *Techniques of Kiln-formed Glass* by Keith Cummings is the classic text on the subject.

CASE STUDY: GOSHKA BIALEK

Bialek deals with the body in her glass sculpture. The transfer prints show a range of representations of the body throughout history. During casting, the prints move and distort with the glass. In the finished work the printed figures appear to 'swim' within the glass form.

MA student Goshka Bialek applies transfers to ingots of casting glass.

Newspaper, Goshka Bialek, Poland, 2003. Kiln formed glass with transfer print inclusions, 200 x 60 x 40 cm including stand. Photographer: Tim Adams.

After firing on the transfer, she lays the ingots into a plaster and molochite mould, which is cast in the kiln at around 850°C.

CASE STUDY: KEVIN PETRIE

In this piece the narcissus-like mask form makes reference to a boat, a metaphor for the journey through life. The transfer print shows a shadowy face passing though inside, like a memory. A drawing of a face was printed in black ceramic enamel onto transfer paper. Once dry, this was overprinted with white and, when this was dry, another face in black was printed on top. The print was sandwiched between two sheets of float glass after firing on, then fused and slumped. In the finished piece both faces can be viewed through the glass. Ceramic enamel was used as it is more likely than glass enamel to withstand the firing temperatures of around 800°C needed to slump the glass.

Voyage, Kevin Petrie, UK, 1995. Kiln-formed glass mask with transfer-printed inclusion, mirror and concrete base, 20 x 30 x 30 cm.

This piece shows a personality made up of several disparate elements. Transfer prints from drawings were cut up and applied to square and rectangular pieces of glass. More glass was fused on top to sandwich the prints. These pieces were then laid into a plaster/molochite mould and fused and slumped together to create the mask form.

Photofit, Kevin Petrie, UK, 1995. Kiln-formed glass mask with transfer-printed inclusion, mirror and concrete base, 20 x 30 x 30 cm.

CASE STUDY: DEVI KHAKHRIA

Designer and artist Khakhria had sheets of transfers printed, including graduated colour blends. She then cut and collaged the sheets and applied them to glass. The transfers were fired on and the glass slumped into moulds to form the dish shapes.

Four plates from the *Jazz* designs series, Devi Khakhria, UK, 1993. Screenprinted transfers on glass, 25 cm diameter.

CASE STUDY: KATHRYN HODGKINSON

Created as part of a residency at Killhope Lead Mining Museum in the UK, the imagery for this piece was taken from photographs of the woods at Killhope. Hodgkinson was interested in freezing a moment in time. Photography has always been an important tool in her work, initially as a means to gather information and more recently as a medium to combine directly with glass. She is interested in using selection to extract minute details from the chaos of the everyday, and glass/photography as a means to represent the abstracted imagery. Transfer prints of Hodgkinson's photographs were made by a transfer-printing firm. To make the piece, two separate pieces of glass were cast and fully polished. The transfers were then applied and the glass pieces refired in a mould, trapping the printed images between the glass. The transfer prints were deliberately not fired on between firings. This meant that when the medium and covercoat burned off, the photographic image was distorted.

Reflection 2, Kathryn Hodgkinson, UK, 2003. Kiln-formed glass with transfer-print inclusions, 26 x 18 x 5 cm.

There are several ways to combine transfers with kiln glass. Transfers can be applied to pieces of float (window) glass and fired on. Another piece of glass can then be placed on top and fused to the first in the kiln. This will encase the image between the two sheets of glass. Further pieces of glass and prints can be added to create depth. Of course, this technique can also be applied with direct-printed sheets of glass. Having sandwiched a print between two sheets of glass and fused them together, this can then be slumped into a dish-shaped mould in the kiln to create a plate shape.

Custom-run and open-stock transfers

If you do not have access to printing facilities or you need a large number of transfers, perhaps for production ware, you can get a firm to make custom sheets of transfers for you. To do this you would either send an image on paper – maybe a drawing, photograph, or lettering – or artwork on disk to the company. They will then make the screens, print the transfers and send you back sheets that you can cut out and apply and fire onto glass yourself. You will have to specify what sort of enamel you need the image to be printed in – glass or ceramic. The more sheets that you get printed the cheaper this option will be. For one or two sheets it can be rather expensive.

As well as getting transfers made of your own artwork, you can also buy ready-printed designs from manufacturers. These are usually of a decorative nature, floral designs being especially common. Catalogues are available that you can select from. The designs can then be applied to the objects of your choice. Such open-stock transfers are normally used to decorate production ware, but are sometimes used for more ironic or subversive purposes. They could also be cut up and collaged onto glass.

CASE STUDY: EFFIE BURNS

Architectural glass artist Burns made a series of tiles for the Early Years Excellence Centre, Hadston, UK. She had photographs of parents and children from the centre made into transfers by transfer-print manufacturer (see Pamela Moreton Ltd in the UK or BelDecal.com in the USA). Usually, you would apply the transfer and fire it onto the glass to allow the covercoat and printing medium to burn away before fusing another piece on top. In this case, when Burns assembled the tiles the pieces of glass and the rod-like stringers lifted the clear piece of glass away from the transfer. This allowed the medium and covercoat to burn away before the glass melted down onto the transfers and trapped them inside.

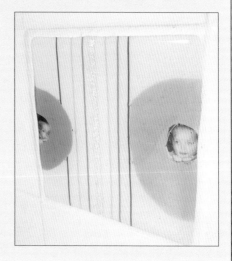

Fused glass tile, Effie Burns, UK, 2001. White Bullseye glass with stringers and transfers with a clear layer of Bullseye glass fused on top. Photographer: David Lawson.

CHAPTER SIX

RELIEF PRINTING

This chapter focuses on printing and casting glass from linocuts and other relief-printing blocks. It also describes how to make photopolymer plates, which allow for a greater variety of imagery to be reproduced.

What is relief printing?

Relief printing usually involves a flat surface, such as a sheet of lino or wood, from which areas are cut away to leave a raised design in relief. This is then rolled with a layer of ink and printed under pressure onto paper in a relief press. In the absence of a press, paper can be placed onto the inked relief block and the back burnished with a baren (a spoon is an effective alternative) to transfer the ink image to the paper. For further details on relief printing for paper see *Relief Printing* by Ann Westley or, if you can find a copy, the classic *Linocuts and Woodcuts* by Michael Rothenstein.

MA student Daniel Savage cutting a lino block. He has drawn the image to be printed with black marker pen and is removing the unwanted areas with a linocutting tool.

You might also consider making your own rubber stamps by cutting into the surface of a pencil eraser using a sharp knife. This can then be

A test piece of float glass, relief-printed from materials found around the studio. Clockwise from top left: lino, press print (available from art shops), a block of polystyrene packaging, a piece of mould-making material.

printed in the same manner as a linocut. Commercially produced rubber stamps can be used in the same way. In fact, any surface that can be inked up with a roller might form a potential relief-printing surface. Try silicon rubber sheets, polystyrene, fabric, or even cut potatoes, turnips or swede.

Window Lights, Mike Davis, UK, 1969. Leaded glass printed with silver stain from linocuts. For this early excursion into printing by a glass artist, Davis printed silver stain from lino blocks using a printing press.

Relief printing and glass

Relief printing is a useful approach for printing onto glass because imagery and texture can be achieved without the need for expensive printing equipment. The tools for relief printing are so compact that you can have your 'print studio' in a shoebox. Linocuts can be printed onto glass directly by hand or by using a traditional relief-printing press. Plaster moulds can also be taken from relief blocks, into which glass can be cast to create a relief surface.

To make the ink for relief printing, enamels can be mixed with a medium such as a clove oil-based universal printing medium, available from ceramic- and glass-enamel suppliers. You might also try a number of mediums used for printing onto paper, for example, lithographic extender base, or transparent base, or a rubber-based ink such as Van Son. These are available from general printmaking suppliers. Mix the enamel and medium together and then use a muller on sandblasted glass to form a homogenous ink. Traditional glass mediums such as silver stain can also be used.

When using a press to print from a relief block there is a danger that the glass will be broken under pressure,

CASE STUDY: PHILIPPA BEVERIDGE

Barcelona-based artist Philippa Beveridge exploits the potential of linocuts to great effect. As well as printing directly from lino onto glass, she also makes casts from linocuts. Beveridge makes architectural commissions, installations and sculpture using glass and other materials. She often employs printing techniques in her work, sometimes using the glass itself to print with, so that the glass exists both as an object but also as a 'trace' or reminder.

Expansive Memory, Philippa Beveridge, UK/Spain, 2002. Detail from an architectural panel, lino printing, silver staining and sandblasting, 70 x 30 x 0.5 cm.

When printing silver stain, Beveridge prints straight from a lino block, without a press. She either mixes the silver stain directly onto the sheet of glass to be used for the final piece, or uses a different sheet of glass as a palette. The lino is used to 'take away' the silver stain from the piece, leaving the clear areas, or, having pressed it down onto the palette, to print the image on another piece of glass. In this case both methods are used to build up the layered image.

For pieces such as this, Beveridge cuts the image into lino, and then takes a plaster mould into which she pours hot wax. She makes several casts, soaking the mould in water in between, and then 'solders' them together by heating a wax-carving tool with a blowtorch. She then makes a plaster/silica mould around the wax and melts it out. Chunks of casting glass (in this case it was a 25 per cent lead-crystal glass) are then added to the mould and cast in the kiln.

Longing Desire, installation detail, Philippa Beveridge, UK/Spain, 2002. Lost-wax cast glass with cold working, 105 x 55 x 1.5 cm. Photographer: Philippa Beveridge.

so it is important to ensure that the printing bed is flat and the glass carefully packed with printing blankets. Some trial and error may be needed to establish the correct pressure. If you want to print by hand, just ink up the lino with a roller, then press the block ink side down against the surface of the glass. You might also try rolling or screenprinting a flat area of ink directly onto the glass and then using a linocut to 'lift' areas of the ink away. Again, some experimentation will be needed in terms of ink consistency and pressure.

Photopolymer-plate printing (flexography)

This method offers an alternative to hand-cut relief-printing plates and allows for a greater range of imagery to be reproduced, including photographic and computer-generated images. Photopolymer-plate printing, sometimes known as flexography or solarplate printing, is a commercial process commonly used for printing packaging. The plate is exposed to ultraviolet light (sunlight can be used) and developed in warm water. This produces a printing plate with a relief surface of between 1 and 4 mm. Conventionally, ink is applied to the plate either on the uppermost surface (relief printing) or in the depressed areas (intaglio printing) and the image is printed onto paper.

A photopolymer plate consists of a backing sheet, usually of steel or aluminium, a photosensitive polymer layer that hardens when exposed to ultraviolet light, and an adhesive layer that bonds the polymer to the backing sheet and prevents light reflection. The surface of the polymer layer is protected with a cover film that must be removed before use.

For printing onto glass you can roll up the surface of a photopolymer plate with ink and print as you would a linocut. You could also try printing the plate like an etching (see Chapter 8). Chapter 7 discusses another approach using photopolymer plates involving taking plaster moulds from the plates

into which glass can be cast to form designs in relief. For further information on photopolymer-plate printing for paper, see *Printmaking with Photopolymer Plates* by Diane Longley

Float glass, relief printed in black from an intaglio photopolymer plate. Kevin Petrie.

Preparing photopolymer plates

As the plates are light-sensitive you must remember to keep them out of strong light for prolonged periods before exposure. Prepare a positive/negative of the image that you want to print. This can be hand-drawn, a scanned image or computer-generated. Use a negative for relief printing and a positive to make an intaglio plate. Cut the plate to an appropriate size with tin snips. You should leave a gap of at least 1 cm between the edge of the plate and the edge of the image.

1 (above, left) Remove the protective plastic cover film from the plate.

2 (above, right) Place the plate face up onto the exposure unit. Place the positive/ negative, reading the right way, onto the plate. Operate the vacuum, if available, to

secure the plate and artwork in position. Expose the plate. In this case a setting of 40 light units is used, though, this will vary depending on the nature of your exposure unit. Therefore, it would be wise to carry out some tests to establish the correct exposure time so as to provide the sharpest image.

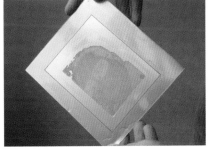

3 Having exposed the plate, remove it from the unit and transfer it to a tray of warm water in subdued lighting. Systematically work over the plate with a soft, flat brush (a paint pad for decorating is ideal) to wash away the unwanted polymer from the plate. This should be done gently to avoid washing away parts of the image.

4 You should aim to reach the steel base of the plate in the non-image areas for a relief plate, and vice versa for an intaglio plate. When the plate is fully cleaned, blot away the excess water with some newspaper and leave to dry thoroughly in a warm place. A drying cabinet used for screenprinting is ideal. Once dry, place the protective cover film back onto the plate and re-expose to ultraviolet light to fully harden the plate.

CHAPTER SEVEN

INTEGRATED GLASS PRINTS

A potential new method of working, developed by the author, that combines photopolymer-plate printing with kiln glass to create pieces in which the 'print' and glass are fully integrated.

Combining kiln-formed glass and intaglio printmaking

This chapter relates to a research project, funded by the Arts and Humanities Research Board (AHRB), initially undertaken in the Glass and Ceramics Department at the University of Sunderland, with additional work at the Centre for Fine Print Research, University of the West of England (UWE).

The project developed a method of working for glass artists and printmakers that combines practical working methods derived from two separate branches of the creative arts: kiln-formed glass (*pâte de verre*) and intaglio printmaking (photopolymer plates or flexography, see Chapter 6).

The project investigated the potential for creating shallow plaster moulds from flexography plates into which glass frit could be cast to form sheets with raised designs. Fine glass frit is applied to the intaglio areas of the mould to form a line image. Coloured glass powders are then sieved into the mould to create areas of colour. A slightly coarser layer of clear frit is subsequently added for strength. The glass filled mould is then fired in the kiln to produce high-quality repeatable panels of glass with an integrated design. These can also be slumped in a mould in a kiln to create dish forms. Further research will explore the potential for shaping these sheets into three-dimensional forms using 'hot glass' techniques.

The advantage of using glass with a relief surface as opposed to other materials, such as ceramic, is that it allows a greater transmission of light. Consequently, this research project may ultimately have relevance for architectural applications where permanency, light transmission and efficiency of production are important. It also offers a new creative opportunity for the production of autonomous panel and decorative objects.

For more details on the specific aims and stages of the initial project, and firing details, see 'Integrated Glass Prints' in the 'Research Projects' section of 'Learning about Glass' on the Gateway to Glass website: www.gatewaytoglass.org.

Wearside view, Kevin Petrie, UK, 2004. Integrated glass print made with Bullseye frit, 29 x 21 cm.

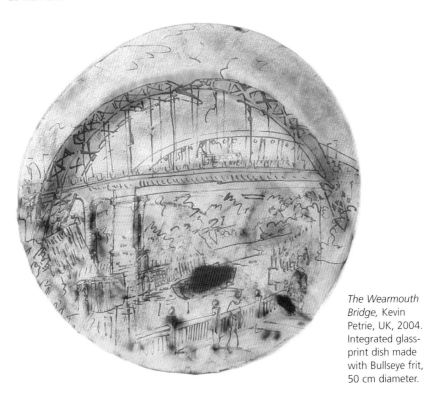

The Wearmouth Bridge, Kevin Petrie, UK, 2004. Integrated glass-print dish made with Bullseye frit, 50 cm diameter.

Stages of making an integrated glass print

1 A number of drawings of the subject matter are made first, in order to 'introduce' the subject. These are used when applying the glass to a mould, for information on colour and the general 'feel' of the piece. A pen-and-ink drawing is then made, again directly from the subject onto acetate. This forms the positive for print.

2 A photopolymer plate is exposed to ultra-violet light using this hand-drawn positive and washed out as described in the Chapter 6. Printight plates from Toyobo can be used. Both the KM152R (relief depth of 1.22 mm) and the KM95R (relief depth of 0.65 mm) are effective. The greater the relief depth, the thicker and darker your line image will be. In this case we are left with an intaglio plate, as a positive (as opposed to negative) image was used. A silicone-rubber cast is now taken from the plate. First a reservoir is made to contain the silicone. Here, thick form board has been used.

3 Mix the silicone according to the manu-facturers instructions. Paint a layer of silicone onto the plate, making sure that all the intaglio areas are filled. Pour in the rest of the silicone up to a level of about 1 cm and leave to cure.

4 Carefully remove the silicone and trim the edges if necessary. We now have a model of the plate from which numerous moulds can be taken, and into which glass can be cast to create repeatable 'prints'.

5 Spray-Mount the silicone-rubber cast to a flat table. Make a reservoir of clay to contain the plaster and molochite mix (1 lb plaster:1 lb molochite:1 pint water). Paint on the plaster mix to ensure that all the detail is picked up, then pour in the rest of the mix.

6 Once the plaster is dry, trim any rough edges to prevent contamination of the glass. Carefully remove the silicone. We now have a plaster mould with an intaglio design to which glass can be applied. Thoroughly dry the mould before applying glass. Wearing a mask, apply powdered glass frit into the intaglio areas of the mould with a piece of stiff card. In this case, fine black frit from Bullseye Glass Co. is used to create the lines.

7 Once the depressed areas of the design are filled, sieve the colour into the mould. Once the colour is applied, add both clear and opaque frit in a slightly coarser grain size to add strength. Areas of clear and opaque frit are used to control the transmission of light through the piece.

8 The loaded mould is placed in a kiln and fired. You can see here that after firing the piece becomes more translucent.

9 The finished piece. In this case the flat print has been slumped into a dish form in a plaster mould in a second firing.

CASE STUDY: KEVIN PETRIE

'Drawing has always formed a central strand of my practice. Over the years I have explored a range of methods to translate the experience of specific places, events and people through drawing into a permanent state, thus "fixing" the experience. This has involved making objects in ceramic, glass and enamel to form a context for the drawn image. Printing has been used as means of transferring the drawn image to the object.

'The development of integrated glass printing enabled me to bring together my interests in drawing, printing and object-making to create celebratory objects. The fact that the pieces are translucent adds a dimension not possible with other media. As light passes through them the pieces are "brought to life". They also change as the light changes. This gives a sense of passing time, adding an

important contrast to the "fixed moment" as recorded in the drawn, printed image. Both opaque and transparent glass can be used to modify the transmission of light.'

Wearside view (detail), Kevin Petrie, UK, 2004. Integrated glass print made with Bullseye frit, 29 x 21 cm. Note the relief surface of the black-line areas.

Wearmouth Bridge, Pastel and watercolour, 2004

The Wearmouth Bridge (detail), 2004. Integrated glass-print dish made with Bullseye frit, 50 cm diameter. Note how light is allowed through the areas in the sky where clear frit has been used, and how it is blocked by areas of opaque frit, for example, in the green of the bridge.

CHAPTER EIGHT

PRINTING FROM AN ETCHING PLATE ONTO GLASS

Not to be confused with etching the glass itself, this chapter revisits methods similar to early printing onto glass from metal plates to offer an alternative form of aesthetic.

Decanter and stopper, 1825–30, Russian, printed and gilt purple glass.
Collection of the Victoria and Albert Museum, London.
Photo: V&A Images.

Engraving and etching

The first methods for printing onto glass used engraved copperplates (see Chapter 1). The plates were inked up with colour that could withstand heat, and then printed into a special tissue. The printed tissue was applied to the glass, ink side down, and the back rubbed to offset the image onto the object. It was then fired to fix the image. There a number of examples of glass printed from metal plates from the eighteenth and nineteenth centuries in museum collections, but few contemporary examples. In this chapter, we will revisit this aesthetic through the use of etching, a similar method to engraving. This provides an additional glass-and-print method that might be used by today's artists.

Engraving is a difficult print process to master. However, similar effects can be achieved with etching, which is a little easier. Etching involves biting a design into the surface of a metal plate with acid. This creates an intaglio surface, meaning that the design is depressed into the surface of the plate. Ink is applied to this surface and printed onto paper under pressure through an etching press.

Lamp, Central Europe, 1850, full view and detail. Note that the delicate black print has been overpainted with coloured enamels. Museum of Decorative Arts in Prague.
Photo: Gabriel Urbánek.

Printing etchings onto glass does not appear to be a widely used technique at present. It can be a rather tricky process and does not have such predictable results as screenprinting. Having said that, it does offer a distinctive and delicate aesthetic in its own right. Etchings can be applied to both flat and three-dimensional forms.

The process works especially well on white or opal glass, as this helps to show up the delicate print. This is also seen on early examples of printed glass. Etching onto glass might be of special interest to printmakers who use etching and want to try printing their plates onto glass. You should bear in mind that an etching printed onto glass will rarely be as fine as one printed onto paper. It should also be noted that hard-ground line etchings are the kind most suitable for printing onto glass. An aquatint, a process that provides a tonal image, is unlikely to work as well.

As with many of the processes described in this book, etching is a very broad subject, and if you are unfamiliar with it you are advised to seek some expert guidance in the first instance. The step-by-step guide below can only provide a basic overview of the subject, and some knowledge of etching is assumed. It is also assumed that access to a fully equipped etching studio is possible. As with any print process you must carefully adhere to all health and safety guidance given on any products that you use.

Making a hard-ground etching plate and printing from it onto glass

1 First file the edges of the plate diagonally at an angle of 45° to remove the shape edge. This ensures that the printing press will not be damaged during printing. The plate must then be thoroughly degreased by rubbing the surface well with vinegar and talc. You will know when the plate has been degreased, as water will not be repelled from the surface. Place the plate on a hotplate and apply some hard ground. This is a wax-like substance that will resist the action of acid. Roll the hard ground over the plate to create an even surface.

2 Draw the design through the hard ground to reveal the metal plate. The exposed areas of the plate will be bitten by acid to create an intaglio design. The hard ground will resist the non-image areas.

3 Wearing goggles and gloves, place the plate in the acid (ferric chloride). You must follow all health and safety guidance when using any printmaking or glass material. The biting time will depend on the strength of the acid. The plate can be removed and the image checked during biting. Remove the plate

PRINTING FROM AN ETCHING PLATE ONTO GLASS

1 Applying a hard ground.

2 Drawing the image through the ground.

3 Placing the plate in the acid (ferric chloride).

4 Inking the plate.

5 The plate on the press.

6 Removing the printed paper.

7 Transferring the print.

8 Carefully removing the potter's tissue.

An etching printed onto white opal Bullseye glass.

from the acid and carefully wash the plate. Again, you must wear suitable protective clothing. Use white spirit to remove the hard ground.

4 To prepare the ink, mix medium copperplate oil and glass enamels. Wear a mask when using enamels. Use a muller on sandblasted glass to create a homogenous consistency. You should aim for thick ink. Using a stiff piece of card, apply the ink to the intaglio areas of the plate. Take a ball of etching scrim and wipe the excess ink from the surface of the plate, leaving ink in the depressed areas of the design.

5 Place the plate onto the bed of the etching press. Put a piece of 'potter's tissue' on top and then a damp piece of paper. Gently cover with the blankets and run through the press.

6 Carefully remove the printed paper from the plate. Separate the potter's tissue from the damp paper.

7 Carefully place the printed tissue onto the glass. Gently rub the back of the tissue with your fingers and then with a rubber kidney as used by potters. A little soft soap or liquid soap can be used as a lubricant at this stage.

8 Slowly remove the tissue. When dry, fire the image on. The temperature will depend on the nature of the colour that you have used. If a glass enamel is used the firing temperature is likely to be between 550 and 590°C (1022-1094°F).

CHAPTER NINE

RESISTS FOR SANDBLASTING

These films resist the action of the sandblaster, allowing for detailed imagery to be applied to the surface of the glass. They even allow for deep sandblasting into the glass. In this chapter, artist Karin Walland describes her creative approach to using resists for sandblasting.

Dress 2, Helen Maurer, 1994, sandblasted glass. The image was taken from a family photograph and blown up to life-size. A sandblast resist was applied to the glass and it was sandblasted at a very low pressure to retain the fine detail. Photographer: Helen Maurer.

Sandblast resists

The special ultraviolet-sensitive sandblast resist was initially developed for monumental masons. For creative purposes it was first used for fine art printmaking to make photographic woodcut printing blocks, a technique known as 'helio relief'. From a personal perspective it was useful for expressing 'memory' through the creation of multilayered images. As glass already possesses two visible surfaces to be exploited, it seemed an obvious method to exploit, enabling the obscuring, revealing and overlapping of fragments of pictures.

To form a coating that is resistant to sandblasting, a rubber-like ultraviolet-sensitive material is applied to the surface of the glass. When exposed to ultraviolet light this material (either in the form of an emulsion applied to glass or a rubberised film sandwiched between two layers of polythene) will harden where the light strikes. In order to create the image a positive or negative is used, rather like when making a stencil for screenprinting. Where the positive or negative blocks the light, the resist remains soft and can be washed off using a pressure washer or a pressure hose. The choice of wash facility depends on which resist material is used. Anything that is dense enough to block the ultraviolet light is usable as a black-out material. This could be photographic film, laser or ink-jet printouts, cut-out card stencils, hand-drawn artwork on drafting film or True-Grain, oiled photocopies or a type of paper known as vellum. The range of options is similar to that of screenprinting, so transferring photographs is not the only one (see Chapter 3 for more details on making artwork for print).

An outline of the possible advantages and disadvantages of the different resists is given below. The choice is a matter of personal preference and depends on the development of the artwork. Two different approaches are described in detail, the SBX liquid emulsion and APM Plus self-adhesive film. For detailed information about all the different types of film contact the suppliers listed at the end of the book. They are very helpful and have excellent support services and websites.

Liquid emulsion

The SBX liquid emulsion consists of a mixture of a stock solution and an activator. The advantages of using liquid emulsions as a sandblast resist are as follows:

- The stock solution lasts for 12 months and the activator lasts almost indefinitely if stored in a freezer.
- The emulsion is applied directly to the surface of the item that is going to

be sandblasted, either with a hard squeegee, or with a screenprinting coating trough, or it can be sprayed on. The latter makes it ideal for complicated surfaces or for large pieces.

- It is perhaps the best resist for deep sandblasting and makes it possible to blast deeply into or even right through a sheet of glass.
- It is the least ultraviolet-sensitive of all the sandblast resists. Consequently, the application need not take place in darkroom conditions. In fact, because of this low light sensitivity, SBX liquid can be exposed in sunlight. However, as the drying involves a rather longer period than the films, it needs to be dried in the dark.
- It is economical for a large output over a short time or for large pieces, as there are restrictions to the size of film sheets available.

The disadvantages of using liquid emulsions as a sandblast resist are as follows:

- It is messy to use and sticks firmly to many surfaces.
- Three-dimensional surfaces must be coated in several thin coats, drying in between.
- It has a limited shelf life once the emulsion and activator

Frozen Dance, Karin Walland, UK, 2003 sandblast resist on glass using a film resist, 9.5 x 28 cm. To create the powerful sense of movement, the resist was stretched and puckered prior to application.

have been mixed (a few weeks, though this can be extended somewhat by keeping it in a refrigerator).
- It can take longer to obtain than some of the films.

Film

There are a number of different films available; most of them are most commonly available in thicknesses of either 75 or 125 microns.

Self-adhesive film
Self-adhesive films offer the following advantages:
- Standard self-adhesive film is readily available and no separate adhesive is called for.
- The films are exposed and developed prior to being applied to the glass. This results in easier handling during exposure.
- Self-adhesive film without washout cuts out two steps in the process, the washout and the drying phase.
- Self-adhesive film without washout has a shelf life of 18 to 24 months.

Again, there are some disadvantages to consider:
- It is possible to damage the adhesive of standard self-adhesive film during the washout process, and it may stick to itself. None of these films will stand up to the prolonged sandblasting that the liquid emulsion will withstand. Therefore, they are less suitable for deep sandblasting.
- Self-adhesive film without washout continues to be sensitive to ultraviolet light at the sandblasting stage, as there is no development phase.
- Self-adhesive film without washout is expensive.

Non-adhesive film
Non-adhesive films offer the following advantages:
- Some of these films have an indefinite lifetime.
- There are no problems of accidentially washing off the adhesive and no problem of it sticking to itself.
- Along with emulsion this can be a very suitable medium for complicated surfaces, as at least one type of this film is very pliable.

Possible disadvantages include:
- It needs a separate adhesive. It can be difficult to apply this evenly and, if applied in too thick a layer, will slow down, or even prevent, sandblasting taking place.

Equipment and materials required for all resists

Image

You will first need an image, or anything else that will block the ultraviolet light; it must have dense blacks (see Chapter 3 for details on making the artwork to create stencils). To get accurate grey tones when sandblasting halftone, images of 35 to 45 dpi must be employed. It is possible to get a gradation of depth of cut by using continuous-tone images, as the less well-developed resist in the grey areas will break up faster than the fully developed. This technique is rather difficult to control, as it needs very careful washout and drying. As a contact-print process is used, the negative (or positive) must be the same size as the final required image.

Ultraviolet light source

Ideally, a 365-nanometer ultraviolet light source (essential for the non-washout film) is required. Screenprinting exposure units are fine for this purpose. The following table is for guidance only, as the precise distances will depend on the age of your light source.

Ultraviolet light sources and their exposure distances	
Light source	**Exposure distance**
Sun (for liquid emulsion only)	1 KW
Mercury vapour	45 cm (18 in.)
Fluorescent (black)	10 cm (4 in.)
3 KW metal halide	80 cm (31 in.)
1 KW metal halide	45 cm (18 in.)

Whatever light source is used, test pieces should be made if the unit is unknown to the user. If a vacuum system is not available, the positive (or negative) must be held in close contact with the resist. It can be held in position with a glass plate and weights.

Perspex/Plexiglas or other clear acrylic sheet is not suitable due to its flexibility and its powerful absorption of ultraviolet light. When exposing either a thick plate or a three-dimensional object, the areas not to be exposed need to be coated with black (lithography ink or any other ink that is thick enough not to run off the object can be used). As an additional precaution it is wise to place the object on a black, non-reflective surface. Most professional exposure units come with a black rubber surface; otherwise, use a piece of black card. Never look directly at an ultraviolet light source.

Washout facility

A pressure washer (with a pressure of 400–1200 psi) is ideal for a washout facility. A spray gun attached to a tap can be used, but this is only suitable for film with little detail. It is not possible to do a washout in running water from a tap.

Drying facility

To dry the resist, a drying cabinet, as used for screenprinting frames, is ideal. A hairdryer or electric fan could also be used. If you are using film, remove as much moisture as possible with a squeegee before drying it by any other means.

Adhesive

This is required for non-adhesive film only and is available from the film supplier. T-Fix Extra as supplied by Sericol Ltd is also suitable.

Sandblasting facility

Sandblasting facilities can be hired and are often available in university glass departments. See your local telephone directory for your nearest facility.

Stencil stripper (for liquid only)

A stripper is used to remove the resist after sandblasting.

Instructions for SBX liquid emulsion

Applying the emulsion

Activate the emulsion, wearing gloves and goggles, according to the instructions on the tub and leave to stand, preferably overnight. The emulsion can stain clothes and equipment when activated, so take care and avoid contact with skin. Thoroughly degrease the glass to be blasted.

To achieve the required thickness of emulsion, as a guide apply layers of masking tape either to the edge of the glass plate or to the squeegee. Using a resist based on four layers of masking tape, it is possible to blast through a 6 mm glass sheet. Pour the emulsion on the sheet a third of the way from one end, and squeegee first to the shorter end and then back to the other end. If the emulsion is applied too close to one end it will just spill off. A coat takes quite a bit of emulsion, and it is not possible to get an even layer if adding more emulsion part way through. A stiff ruler or screenprinting coating trough is the best applicator.

It is also possible to spray on the emulsion, and for three-dimensional objects this is the best way. For spraying, the sensitised emulsion is diluted one part water to three parts emulsion. Use a conventional paint sprayer with a minimum of 40–50 psi. Spray several thin coats for three-dimensional objects, drying the layers in between each coat, or, for sheets of glass, spray until the orange-peel look of the coating disappears. Sheets should be sprayed flat. Dry the emulsion in a dark, dust-free place. The drying can be speeded up with a hairdryer or fan, or by putting the object in a drying cupboard as used in photography or screenprinting. The emulsion shrinks during the drying phase.

Exposure

Liquid emulsion is the least ultraviolet-sensitive of the resists. This makes it possible to expose it in sunlight. See the table below for approximate recommended exposure times.

Recommended exposure times for liquid emulsion		
Light source	**Exposure distance**	**Time**
Sun		1 min
3 KW metal halide	80 cm (31 in.)	2–2.5 min
1 KW mercury vapour	45 cm (18 in.)	5.5 min+
Fluorescent (blue)	10 cm (4 in.)	5 min+
Fluorescent (black)	10 cm (4 in.)	8–9 min+

The above figures are only approximations; exposure tests are essential. Place the emulsion side of the positive/negative against the dry resist coat. Close contact is necessary during exposure. To achieve this, a vacuum unit, as used to expose screenprinting frames, or a glass plate weighted down is necessary. When a vacuum unit is not available or it is not possible to use one, as for three-dimensional objects, black out areas that might interfere with the accurate exposure and place the object on a black, non-reflective surface. Tests must be done with all light sources and thicknesses of emulsion to determine accurate exposure times. Inadequate exposure will cause the emulsion to wash off during development, while excessive exposure will prevent adequate washout.

Development/washout

Place the item in an upright position and spray with a pressure washer in a fan-shaped pattern (minimum 400 psi). Do not concentrate the spray in one place for too long. Using lukewarm water speeds up the process. Do not overwash. Wash until the image develops clear areas of exposed glass; these are the areas that will be sandblasted. Washout is easier if the glass can be fixed as the pressure of the water can make the glass jump around and break.

CASE STUDY: YOKO MACHI

Machi has developed a 'low tech' but highly inventive and effective technique for combining screenprinting and sandblasting to express her feeling of rising spirits at seeing sunshine after rain. Each element of her piece is made of two sheets of glass glued to a circular spacer to create a gap between them. On the front piece she screenprinted the whole surface using an open screen with yellow enamel. This was then fired on. She then put glue onto areas of the yellow enamel and pushed the other piece of glass against it. The two pieces of glass were pulled apart and the glue allowed to dry. She then sandblasted the piece to remove all the yellow enamel except where the glue acted as a resist. On the other piece of glass she screenprinted colour, leaving a clear area with Fablon. She then fused smashed pieces of glass onto this area to create a glittering light and shadow on the front piece.

Sunny Rain, Yoko Machi, Japan, 2002. Multiple hanging piece comprised of glass, printed enamel and ultraviolet glue.

After development, the object should be dried before sandblasting. It can be heat-dried with a hairdryer or in a heated cabinet. This might cause a slight bubbling of the emulsion, which should not interfere with its ability to withstand blasting.

Sandblasting
Blast at a distance of 15–20 cm (6-8 in.) from the object (20–25 psi for a pressure-pot system and 60–80 psi for a siphon system) holding the gun perpendicular to the surface. Use either pure aluminium oxide or silicon carbide with a grit size of 150–180 depending on how fine the details of the image are. Keep checking the blast.

Stripping the resist

Areas of resist can be peeled off by hand to enable deeper blasting or recoating. For the final strip there is a special SBX stripper available, but it is also possible to use a stripping paste as used to strip emulsion off a screenprinting mesh. Do not leave the stripping paste to go dry, and make sure you wear eye protection when washing off the paste.

Instructions for APM Plus film

The choice of sandblast-resist film will depend on personal preference. All of them work in broadly the same way. APM Plus self-adhesive film is perhaps the most readily available. It is a self-adhesive sandblast resist produced by AICELLO Chemical. It consists of a resist sandwiched between two protective layers, a shiny carrier sheet and a matt slip sheet. The difference is easy to spot when looking at the full sheets in good light, but much more difficult when smaller offcuts are used in low light intensity. To differentiate it is wise to mark the shiny side of smaller pieces of film, as the difference is crucial for development and washout. When stored in a dry and cool environment APM Plus has a shelf life of 12 months.

Exposure

Expose APM Plus with the emulsion side of the negative/positive facing the matt slip sheet, using a vacuum exposure unit or keeping the negative in close contact with the APM Plus by weighing it down with a heavy sheet of glass. The figures given in the table below are guidelines only; exposure tests will be required for all exposure units.

Recommended exposure times for self-adhesive film			
Light source	**Exposure distance**	**75 micron exposure time**	**125 micron exposure time**
3 KW metal halide	80 cm (31 in.)	20–30 sec	30–40 sec
1 KW mercury vapour	45 cm (18 in.)	30–50 sec	45–60 sec
Fluorescent (black)	10 cm (4 in.)	60–80 sec	90–110 sec

Washout/development

Remove the slip sheet from the APM Plus. This can be a fiddly process. It can be aided by applying a piece of tape to either side of the APM Plus and gently pulling apart. It is wise to practise this before attempting important pieces.

Position the film in a vertical position, either clamped onto a heavy sheet of glass or taped to the glass plate with heavy-duty tape to prevent the spray

CASE STUDY: BINITA WALIA

Stairtower with Skywindows, Binita Walia, UK, 2003. Sandblasted glass with appliquéd coloured glass squares. © Mode 1 Architects. Skywindows made by Goddard & Gibbs.

These windows, part of the refurbishment of Angell Town Housing Estate in London, show an alternative method of sandblast resist. In this case a resist has been screenprinted onto the glass, as opposed to a film or coating applied to the glass, and then exposed to ultraviolet light. After sandblasting the resist was removed and the coloured glass squares were glued into place. Walia says of this piece, 'My brief was to create art for all. Sky is a recurring image in my work and symbolises that we are all the same and all live under one sky. I also aimed to generate harmony and calm for the residents'.

flapping the film around, which could cause damage to the self-adhesive or cause the film to stick to itself or stretch out of shape.

Wash out the film with a pressure hose or pressure washer. Spray in a slow, even motion, avoiding focusing the spray for too long on any one point. Halftones take longer to wash out. Extended washout can damage both the adhesive and the detail of the image.

Following washout the mask needs to be dried prior to attaching it to the glass. First remove excess water with a squeegee, then the rest of the drying can be carried out in a heated cabinet or with the aid of a hairdryer.

Application

It is wise to put registration marks, complete with a centre mark on the glass and a centre mark on the carrier sheet of the film, prior to applying the sandblast film to the glass, as it is very difficult to reposition the APM Plus.

However, there are films on the market that can be repositioned. With the carrier sheet facing you, match the two centre marks and smooth out the film from the centre towards the sides to avoid trapping air bubbles that could easily break during the blasting and ruin the image. Once the film is applied, it needs to be burnished to give overall adhesion. First use your fingers and then something like a blending stick as used in pastel drawing. Burnishing is especially important for halftone images to ensure a detailed image. Finally, remove the shiny carrier sheet, making sure to burnish carefully where you started the peel-off, as the carrier sheet can be difficult to separate from the film, and the film might lift off a bit where you started the separation.

Sandblasting

The manufacturers recommend blasting at a distance of 15-20 cm (6-8 in.) from the object (20-25 psi for a pressure-pot system and 60-80 psi for a siphon system), holding the gun perpendicular to the surface. A coarser grit and higher pressure can be used for more texture and higher penetration.

Use either pure aluminium oxide or silicon carbide with a grit size of 150-180 depending on how fine the details of the image are. Keep checking the blast. It is possible to remove part of the resist during the process to add new areas to be blasted in stages.

Removal of mask

The resist can be either peeled off the glass or removed by soaking in tap water for 15-20 minutes.

1 Exposure of the film.

2 Peeling off the protective backing.

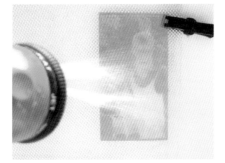

3 Washing out the film.

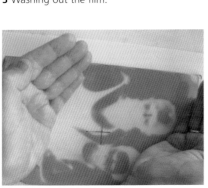

4 Applying the film to glass.

5 The sandblasted glass, *Father and Child* by Karin Walland.

CHAPTER TEN

RESISTS FOR ETCHING GLASS

Etching glass involves the use of acid or similar products to 'bite' designs into the surface of glass. This chapter focuses on resists for etching paste. If only a surface frosting is required this method is often the most practical and economic.

A word on safety

Various methods can be used to mask areas of the glass to create the acid-etched design. Acid-etching can involve the use of hydrofluoric or nitric acid to give deep bites. Both are subject to very strict health and safety guidance and are beyond the scope of this book, so if you are unfamiliar with acid-etching for glass you should seek expert training in a properly equipped facility.

The use of acid-etching paste, described by Karin Walland below, is a less dangerous way to produce a shallow etch than with hydrofluoric or nitric acid. Having said that, the manufacturer's health and safety guidelines should still be strictly adhered to. Glass-etching pastes can also be screenprinted. Mico Printing Supplies Ltd (London, UK) stocks glass-etching products for screenprinting.

Simple printed resists

Simple resists for acid-etching can be created with the use of bitumen, Brunswick black or Rhinds turpentine based stop out varnish, as used when making etchings from metal plates. Bitumen can be purchased from hardware stores and stop-out varnish from printmaking suppliers. Brunswick black is a product used by sculptors for masking metal. These types of resist can be painted onto the glass and should be allowed to dry before acid-etching. They will resist the acid and can be cleaned off with solvent afterwards to reveal unetched areas of glass. A form of monoprinting can also be used. Paint the bitumen or stop-out varnish onto paper and, while it is still wet, stick it onto a sheet of glass and rub the back of the paper. Some of the resist will 'offset' onto the glass and can create very painterly effects.

CASE STUDY: BRIDGET JONES

Printmaking is central to the work of architectural glass artist Bridget Jones. She uses monoprinting, intaglio and relief printing to generate designs for stained-glass and screenprinted-glass commissions. These are then made on a large scale by a fabricator. She uses monoprinted resists for smaller scale projects.

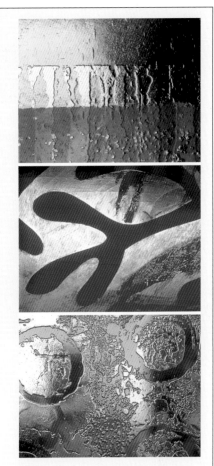

Details of acid-etched, antique flashed glass using monoprinted bitumen as a resist, Bridget Jones, UK. Photographers (from top): David Lawson, David Williams, David Lawson.

Screenprinted resists

Resists can also be screenprinted onto glass. Artwork and screens are prepared as normal, but instead of printing ink onto the glass, the resist is used. Remember to think about whether a negative or positive image should be printed, as the acid will etch in the areas not covered by the resist. It is usually necessary to allow the bitumen to thicken to the consistency of single cream in the open air before printing. The addition of paint dryers can aid the thickening. You should make sure that the glass is completely clean to avoid residue grease resisting the bitumen or varnish. Most of the artists below used either hydrofluoric or nitric acid to bite the glass. After printing, leave the resist to thoroughly dry. After etching, remove the remaining resist with white spirit or turps substitute, then soap and water.

CASE STUDY: HELEN MAURER

This is a shaped mirror that has had the protective backing removed with paint stripper. An image of the wing has been screenprinted onto it using bitumen. The mirror was then acid-etched using nitric acid. The shelf is spotlit to produce the light image above and the shadow below. The image has also been distressed to give it an ethereal quality.

Angel wing 2, Helen Maurer, UK, 1995. Acid-etched mirror and light. Photograph: Helen Maurer.

CASE STUDY: SUNJU PARK

A key component of Park's work is the use of screenprinting with bitumen and then acid-etching, particularly on mirrored surfaces, rather than plain glass. She also makes extensive use of photographic images, either to create detailed images or to provide a textural backdrop to a piece of work with lower-resolution images. The acid-etching of a photographic image converts it from two-dimensional to almost three-dimensional, as the image becomes a relief.

Sunyoung (detail), Sunju Park, South Korea, 2003. Acid-etched mirror and light box, 61 x 26 cm (without light box).

The use of photopolymer film as an acid-paste resist

There are various photopolymer films available from fine art printmaking suppliers that are useful for glass-surface etching with acid-etch paste. ImagOn™ ULTRA (made by DuPont and described in detail below) and PHOTEC, a very similar product made by Hitachi, are examples of films available.

The ImagOn™ ULTRA photopolymer film is sandwiched between a soft, matt peel-back layer that feels a bit like cling film, and a stiffer, shiny Mylar sheet. The importance of the difference between the two covering layers is described below. The photopolymer layer can be laminated onto glass to give an acid resist that can render very fine detail when etched with an etching paste. When the film is exposed to ultraviolet light the molecules struck by the light form polymer chains. This enables the film to withstand the acid in the areas exposed to ultraviolet light, whereas, where the film has been protected from light, it will wash off in the developing solution.

This technique has a lot of advantages over sandblasting if only a surface pattern is required. These include the following:

- Facilities such as pressure washout and a sandblaster are not required. Although the standard UV lamps and screenprinting-emulsion development facilities give a greater degree of control over exposure times, it is also possible to expose the film in sunlight.
- The films are able to render very fine detail, as the developing process is a chemical not a mechanical one, so no consideration needs to be given to the problem of water spray being able to get between halftone dots.
- The film is not as sensitive to light as sandblast resist. The density of the blacks of the transparency is therefore not as crucial (for example, a metal mesh in sunlight can be used as a blocking agent).
- It is substantially cheaper to work with than sandblast resist.

The use of ImagOn™ ULTRA

Working conditions
The film is ultraviolet-sensitive, so it is possible to work safely on the film in low-level ambient light away from sunlight, especially if light sources are covered with a yellow film. It is advisable to cover windows as well if they are not facing north. It might be best to cut and apply the film on dull days or in the evening.

Lamination of the film onto the glass
Clean the glass well so that no grease or cleaning fluid is present on the

surface to be etched. Polish well with a dry cloth or tissue. Cut the film a little larger than required; this also applies if the entire glass surface is to be etched. As the etch is a paste, it is not necessary to cover the entire glass surface if the image is small; it is sufficient to allow for a border of a few centimetres around the image to make sure the paste does not accidentally affect the glass outside the image area.

Remove the soft matt sheet from the film. One of the easiest ways to do this is to fold a bit of adhesive tape with the sticky side outwards and place a corner of the film with the soft matt backing onto the tape. This makes it possible to peel the film off the matt backing sheet. Another way to do it is to rub a corner of the film sandwich between two fingers to separate the layers. The soft inner sheet always makes the film roll up, so when it is removed the film will lie flat.

Place the film with the bare emulsion side face up. Lightly spray the glass surface to be etched with water and then position the film, having flipped it over to bring the film into contact with the glass. The water makes it possible to reposition the film if the registration is not quite right; however, if too much water is applied, the film will slither around on the glass. With the back of your hand, smooth the film from the centre outwards, squeezing out the water and air bubbles in the process. Then do the same with a rubber squeegee, applying ever firmer pressure until no trace of water is left between glass and film.

Dry the laminated film thoroughly with a hairdryer or in a drying cabinet in the same low-level light conditions. Now the film is ready to be exposed. Apart from artwork, it is also possible to use found objects to prevent the light reaching the film, including lace, seed heads and shells.

Exposure

Because of the way ultraviolet light affects the photopolymer film, the areas blocking the light during exposure are the areas that will be etched. In other words, the etch will correspond with the image that you use on your positive or the outline of an item placed on the film.

As stated in Chapter 9, there are a number of possible ultraviolet light sources. It is necessary to do step exposure time tests on any light unit you are not familiar with, as all units vary. Expose the film in 30-second increments up to 5 minutes. That should cover most exposure units. If exposing in sunlight, start at 5 minutes and take the time of day and time of year into account.

For top light exposure, place the glass on a black background with the laminated film face up. Put the transparency on top with the emulsion facing the film emulsion. Finally place a 4–6 mm glass plate on top to ensure close contact between film and transparency, or use a vacuum unit such as a screenprinting exposure unit.

CASE STUDY: JULIAN STOCKS

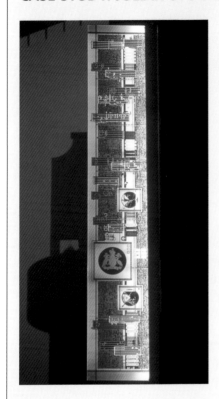

This glass and steel sculpture is integrated into the façade of the Royal Ballet School, London. The design incorporates Benesh notation in the background, a graphic notation used to record movement in dance, as well as extracts from the musical score of the ballet *Sleeping Beauty*. The image shows the piece at night and emphasises the contrasts between the etched areas and the darker screenprinted passages.

Pas de Deux, Julian Stocks, UK, 2003. Clear float glass that has been acid-etched after the screenprinted application of a Brunswick black resist, with additional screenprinted grey two-part epoxy cold-cure ink sandwiched between two sheets of laminated glass, 380 x 70 x 21 cm. Photographer: Julian Stocks.

If the glass is to be put on top of the exposure unit the order is the reverse: put the transparency at the bottom with the emulsion face up, then place the glass plate with the emulsion face down (in this case the weight of the glass itself is enough to get the close contact required between the two emulsions). Finally, the whole thing should be covered with something black. Felt is effective. You are now ready to expose.

If you want a more detailed image with less contrast in the final etch, you can remove the Mylar™ sheet prior to exposure.

Once the film is exposed remove the top, shiny Mylar™ sheet by picking at a corner to lift it off the film, and carefully peel it back, making sure not to lift the film away from the glass. Cutting the film larger than the plate makes this easier to do without damaging the adhesion to the glass. Make sure you check the film has not lifted in the corner where the peel-back of the Mylar started. Now lay the plate upside down with the film at the bottom, and with a very sharp knife cut the film to fit the plate tightly. If this is not done prior to development it is easy to accidentally lift the film in the developing bath, as the same solution is eventually used to completely remove the film from the plate at the end of the process.

Development

In a tray large enough to hold the exposed item dissolve 27 g of washing soda per litre in a small amount of warm water, and top up with cold water (DuPont recommend the use of 10 g of soda ash and considerable precision. Good results can be achieved with very approximate amounts of washing soda, the hydrated form of soda ash (most supermarkets stock it). Wearing gloves, place the exposed item in the tray.

The development is easiest if the solution covers the film; however, with large or awkwardly shaped items it is possible to scoop the solution over it while it develops. The film in the non-exposed areas will thin and wash off after 9–10 minutes if continuously wetted. Alternatively, very gently rub the film, first with the fingers and then with a fine sponge, to speed up the process. Once the unexposed areas of the image are showing completely clear, rinse the item in clean water, dab it with a tissue to remove excess water and dry thoroughly with a hairdryer or in a heating cabinet.

Etching

Place the object to be etched in a large tray or on a surface well covered with newspapers, put on latex or neoprene gloves and wear eye protection. Dab the etching paste all over the image with a brush, making sure there is good covering. Do not brush the paste on unless brushstrokes are specifically required.

Leave the paste on for 10–20 minutes and wash it off with water in the tray before rinsing the item well. If only part of the glass is to be etched, it is advisable before washing to remove excess paste with some tissue from areas not to be etched. A small amount of washing soda added to the wash water in the tray will help neutralise the acid before you dispose of it down the drain. Inspect the etched area. It is possible to apply a new layer of paste if the effect is not dense enough.

It is possible to scrape off some of the paste for reuse before washing the object, but it needs to be done carefully so as not to lift the film prematurely and spread acid onto areas where it is not wanted. Store the used paste in a carefully labelled plastic tub; do not mix it with the unused paste.

Removal of film

Washing soda is used to remove the film. Either soak the film overnight in the developing bath or add more soda to the solution; then wearing appropriate gloves rub the film off.

1 Removing air bubbles and excess water with a squeegee.

2 Washing out the exposed film.

3 Ready to etch.

4 Applying the acid paste.

5 Finished piece *Storm along the Pier* by Karin Walland.

CHAPTER ELEVEN

PHOTOGRAPHY AND GLASS

There is a long tradition of the combination of photography and glass. Although not strictly a printmaking technique, photography does have parallels due to its reproducibility. In this chapter, photographer and glass artist Andrew Conway describes his approach to using photographic emulsion, sometimes known as 'liquid light', on glass.

Early work with photography and glass

Early photographers did not have the benefits of modern gelatin bases for their negatives, so glass was an ideal material due to its smooth surface and translucent qualities. Fragility was always a problem until more flexible and robust materials were developed. As the art and science of photographic imaging has reached a zenith of perfection it has become increasingly difficult for photographers to use modern materials and achieve an original and personal representation of their art.

As mentioned in Chapter 1, there were early experiments of applying photographs to glass and there is still great scope for research in this area. However, for beginners photographic emulsion in a liquid form is a convenient starting point. Most commonly, liquid emulsion has been applied to paper to create painterly effects with photographs. With a little imagination, unusual effects can be achieved by application of the medium to surfaces such as metal, leather or even glass.

Using photographic emulsion with glass

The following is a step-by-step procedure for procuring photographic images on glass surfaces.

Coating photographic emulsion onto glass

1 In order to produce a stable image on glass it is necessary to treat the glass with a layer of varnish. This creates a mordant surface for the emulsion to bite into; in much the same way salt is used in the dyeing of textiles. The glass must be free from grease and dust, which can be achieved by washing it with detergent. Once dry, varnish can be applied to the surface with a

CASE STUDY: ANDREW CONWAY

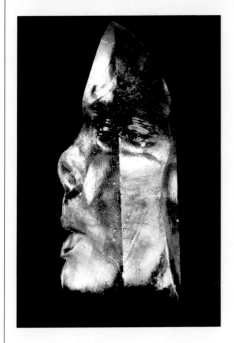

Conway, a relative newcomer to glass, began with the idea of 'auto-icons' (death masks) and has used the self-portrait as a vehicle to explore the possibilities of a 'living memorial'. This piece has a photograph of his face printed onto the glass, using the process described in this chapter. A compelling juxtaposition, is viewable through the glass from many angles, created between the three-dimensional glass head and the surface image.

Self Portrait, Andrew Conway, UK, 2004. Cast glass with photograph, 20 x 5 x 7 cm.

paintbrush, care being taken to give an even covering across the entire surface to be used. The choice of varnish will depend on the desired end result. For instance, it may be that you wish the final image to have a slight tint of colour. Certain varnishes do, of course, have a slightly warm hint. Colour may also be added to the varnish to create colour effects. Clear varnish with a silk finish is ideal. This gives the best surface for the emulsion to grip onto.

2 Once the varnish has completely set, you will need to analyse the quality of the coating. If the coating is uneven it may be necessary to give a second coat or even to discard the piece and begin again. As the varnish dries there is always the danger that dust may attach to the surface, so it is important to work in a dust-free environment. You can set the glass into the bottom of a box lined with damp tissue, and then cover it with a lid. This helps reduce the chances of dust finding its way onto the varnished surface.

3 When you have a surface you are happy with you can then prepare the emulsion. There are several commercially available products, and it is worth experimenting with different products processed in different developers. As the emulsion is in the form of gelatin, it is necessary to warm it up in order to make it fluid. This can be done by placing it on a towel on a radiator or placing the bottle in a bowl of water at a temperature of 45°C for about 20–25 minutes.

4 Once the emulsion has reverted to liquid form you may open the bottle in a darkroom with a red safelight. Liquid emulsion is orthochromatic and so is not affected by red light. Having said that, be careful not to expose it to red light for a prolonged period, as fogging may occur. Pour a small quantity into a cup and replace the lid of the bottle to reduce the risk of fogging the bottle contents.

5 The emulsion may be painted directly onto the varnished glass surface using a soft brush. It is best to use a size 12 sable, though bigger brushes may be used for large-scale application. If you intend to paint straight onto the glass you may find it necessary to apply several layers in order to achieve an even surface. There are two problems with this method. First, the end result is often quite patchy and brush strokes are visible (although you may want this effect). The second problem is with image contrast and density. The thinner the emulsion, the lower the contrast. Blacks tend to be quite washed out, and it is hard to get a good density in shadow areas. If you wish to obtain rich blacks and good tonal range then it is better literally to pour the emulsion onto the glass. Start by pouring slightly more than you need into the centre of the glass and carefully spread it to the edges using a soft round brush. Take note that the brush is used purely to spread the emulsion rather than for painting to the edges.

6 Now that the glass is coated, it will require time to dry in absolute darkness to avoid fogging. If you have poured on the emulsion, it will require a much longer drying time. Do not use a hairdryer to speed up this process, as rapid drying could cause shrink-back or other surface effects. For the drying process, place the glass into a lightproof box and then leave it to set for 24 hours. Once dry, it should have a tough, smooth, white finish.

You now have a suitable photographic plate and can treat it in the same way as you would treat photographic paper. You can print images onto glass using an enlarger, or simply by contact-printing from large-format negatives. There are also endless possibilities for making photograms or other photographic images.

Once you have a coating of photographic emulsion on your glass, it may be treated in the same way as photographic paper, with one or two slight differences. The procedure that follows explains how to enlarge a photograph onto the glass.

Printing images onto glass

1 Once you have chosen a suitable image for enlargement, position the negative into the film holder of the photographic enlarger. To set the size for the intended image, it is useful to have a piece of white card cut to the same size as the glass plate. It is also important to select card of the same thickness as the glass. This ensures that the image will be correctly focused. If the glass you are using varies in thickness across its surface, or if it is a sculptural piece, it may be necessary to stop down the aperture on the lens to increase the depth of field.

2 The next task is to determine the exposure time for the print. For this you will need to have prepared some 'test strips'. These should be strips of glass that have been coated with liquid emulsion using the same process as described earlier. Working in red-safelight conditions, position the test strip under the enlarger so that it crosses the image (make sure that a red safety filter is between the lens and the glass plate).

CASE STUDY: LORNA MCGINTY

This piece forms part of an installation based on the family holiday photographs of MA student McGinty as a child and her late father. The photograph is exposed on the inside of a hot glass-formed 'ball'. The thickness of the glass magnifies the image when viewed from the outside to create an evocative sense of memory.

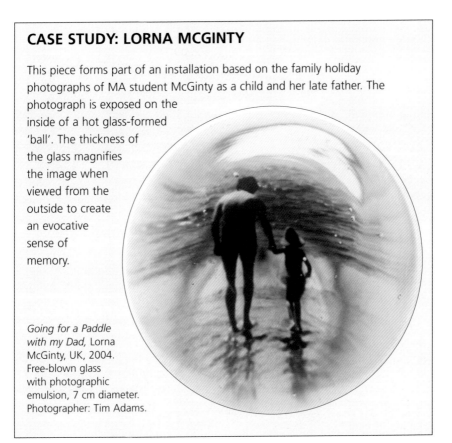

Going for a Paddle with my Dad, Lorna McGinty, UK, 2004. Free-blown glass with photographic emulsion, 7 cm diameter. Photographer: Tim Adams.

3 Once you are happy with the position, switch off the enlarger lamp, remove the safety filter and expose the glass plate to the image for a short, measured period of time. Start with an exposure time of 5 seconds, although this will depend on how bright the image is. Cover a quarter of the test strip with opaque card and make a second exposure for another 5 seconds. Repeat this process until only a quarter of the strip remains uncovered. You now have a glass strip that has four different exposure times along its length from 5 seconds to 20 seconds.

4 Place the test strip into the developer tray. The developer temperature should be between 15-25°C/59-77°F (ideally at 20°C/68°F) and deep enough to cover the glass. Try experimenting with different makes of developer to find the best results for your requirements. Development time can be anywhere between 1 and 3 minutes, although 2 minutes seems adequate with Ilford developers. With variable-contrast photographic papers the contrast is altered by means of filters. This will not work with most liquid-emulsion products, though there is a variable-contrast liquid emulsion available from Rockland Colloid Corp. It is possible to control the contrast in the developer by altering the development time. Less time in the developer gives lower contrast, and maximum development time will give the greatest contrast and density in the blacks. The only problem with this method is that it is quite difficult in safelight conditions to see when you have the desired effect. Too little development may cause flat areas of dark tone to become patchy or milky. To avoid this, allow a minimum time of 30–40 seconds depending upon the chemistry being used.

5 When you feel the image is ready, carefully remove the test strip from the developer and place it in the stop bath. The emulsion is now very delicate due to the absorption of the developer, and is easily scratched. Water may be used in the absence of stop bath.

6 After 20–30 seconds, remove the test strip from the stop bath and place it into the fixer. Once in the fixer, you can put the main light back on. At first the image will appear to have pure white highlights, but as the fixer dissolves the unused emulsion the highlights will become transparent. If you are using white glass the highlights will remain white, but blue glass will give you blue highlights, clear glass will give you clear highlights, etc. Two minutes should be adequate in the fixer, as only the emulsion and not the glass absorbs the developer.

7 You must now wash the test strip. This can be done in a bath of clean water, or run it under a tap gently for a minute or so.

8 Finally, drain off the excess water and leave it to dry. Try to rest the glass at an angle to help the water to drain off easily; this will avoid drying marks. Allow test strips to dry before judging the best exposure time. Contrast and luminosity can dull down slightly once dry, so a more accurate exposure can be obtained. Try to view the test strip in indirect daylight if possible, and select the most effective exposure time. Then, using your main piece of emulsion-coated glass you can make your exposure onto it and repeat steps 4–8.

1 Varnishing the glass.

2 Keep the glass in a box when drying to protect it from dust.

3 Applying the emulsion.

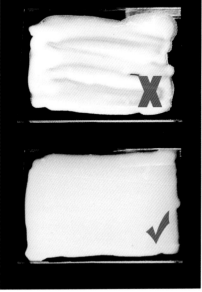

4 Try to achieve an even layer of emulsion.

CHAPTER TWELVE

DIGITAL AND LASER PRINTS

Transfers for glass can be produced from computer printers. These methods are very straightforward but have some limitations. Having said that, they may well form an important and developing strand of glass and print in the future.

Digital printing systems

These systems use a converted digital four-colour printer that prints enamel colours rather than conventional toners. Using the four process colours of cyan, magenta, yellow and black they can produce 256 halftones of colour. The system prints onto A3 (approx. $16^1/_2$ x 12 in.) ceramic water-slide print paper. Transfers can be applied to glass in the same manner as a screenprinted transfer and fired on to form a permanent bond.

The process involved with the production of digital prints is very simple and straightforward. Once an image has been digitised in a suitable format, and at the correct size (remembering that the image size cannot be larger than the print size, unless the image is broken down into smaller-tile size images), it is printed as you would with any other computer print. Ceramic or glass colour is printed onto water-slide paper without any covercoat applied. The company would then use a specially prepared sheet that has a covercoat pre-printed onto a heat-release paper. Both the print paper and the cover paper are passed through a laminator. This transfers the covercoat onto the water-slide sheet. Once complete, the transfer needs to be cut out and immersed in water until you can slide off the image from the backing paper. The image is then applied to the item that is to be decorated, as with a screenprinted transfer.

This process can be used for both glass and ceramic on-glaze decoration, as either a ceramic or glass flux covercoat is applied after printing. You can send the artwork on disk to one of the companies that make digital prints and they will return the finished transfer.

The obvious advantage of this method is that you do not need your own printing equipment and do not have to spend the time learning other print methods. This method is also economic for small numbers of prints. There are, however, some limitations that need to be considered. It is not possible to print white due to the four-colour nature of the process. For ceramic printing

CASE STUDY: ROBERT PRATT MCMACHAN

The images on the glass are produced using high-temperature digital ceramic decals. Pratt McMachan uses bright platinum lustre to 'mirror' out selected figures. They are displayed in deep frames that leave a gap between the printed glass and the 2 mm picture glass in front. The picture glass is screenprinted with acid paste to leave a very lightly etched image. This image is not obvious unless it catches the light, but it throws a shadow back onto the digital print and the backing paper that is quite clear. The transfers are fired onto the glass at about 800°C/1472°F.

Detail from the *Photographic Memory* series, Robert Pratt McMachan, UK, 2004. Mixed media including digital transfers on glass, approximately 35 x 18 cm.

this is rarely a problem as the image is usually applied to white-glazed ceramic objects. Therefore, the white of the image is created by the white object. This is the same in printing four-colour images onto paper. However, when applying the digital prints to transparent glass the areas that should appear white in the image will remain clear. A second issue is that, once fired onto glass, the covercoat layer can leave a visible residue on the glass. This can be alleviated by cutting out the transfer as close to the image as possible. A third difficulty is that the transfers are only available to a maximum size of A3 (approx. $16^{1}/_{2}$ x 12 in.). Having said that, larger-scale pieces can be made

AemAet 2 – Hamepores, Dana Zámečníková, Czech Republic, 2002–3. Acid-etched, digitally enamelled and slumped glass, metal, diameter 170 cm.

by tiling images together. It is also worth noting that additional screenprinted colour can be added to these digital prints.

Laser-printed wet-release decals (Lazertran)

Lazertran was developed in the UK in the mid-1990s by Mick Kelly as an aid to applying and overlaying images on canvas. It was introduced to art schools in workshops where students wanted to apply imagery to other substrates. Kelly endeavoured to develop a product that can be applied to virtually any surface. The image is printed from a conventional laser printer onto the Lazertran. On glass the decal can be applied like a water-slide transfer and fired in a kiln over several hours until it reaches approximately 200°C/392°F. At this point the decal will have melted and become a much more stable and enamel-type coating.

A Lazertran transfer differs from a conventional enamel transfer in that the image is less durable and lightfast. In addition, the colour is less strong, but this can be helped by the addition of a second Lazertran transfer of an identical image applied over the first fired transfer, giving a double density of pigment.

CHAPTER THIRTEEN

'VITREOGRAPHY' PRINTING FROM GLASS ONTO PAPER

The focus of this book is printing onto glass; however, glass can also be used as a printing plate for printing onto paper. This has been developed to a large extent by Harvey Littleton, known as the father of American studio glass, who coined the term 'vitreograph' to describe a print taken from a glass plate.

Printing from glass

The simplest way to take a print from a sheet of glass is to roll up the glass with ink, place a piece of paper on top and then draw a design onto the back of the paper. When the paper is lifted, the ink will have adhered to the paper where pressure was applied. You can also paint or roll ink onto the glass and work directly into it, before placing paper on top and rubbing the back with a baren to achieve a print. Vitreography is different from these forms of monoprinting because the glass is processed to retain the image drawn or painted upon it. As in etching or lithography, a vitreographic image can be reproduced many times, allowing editions to be made.

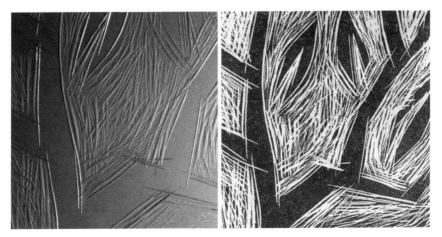

Wheel-engraved glass (left) with a relief print on paper taken from it (right), Bridget Jones, UK. Photographer: David Lawson.

Moonbeam Dancing, Erwin Eisch, Germany, 1991. Vitreograph; three-colour intaglio print from a glass plate. Limited edition of 50 with 16 artist's proofs, hand-printed on Arches acid-free paper. The sheet is 75 x 56 cm and the image is 50 x 40 cm. Numbered and signed by the artist. Printed by Judith O'Rourke. Courtesy of Littleton Studios.

Intaglio and planographic vitreographs

Techniques have been developed for creating both intaglio and planographic vitreographs . The starting point in both processes is a sheet of $^3/_8$ inch (1 cm) thick float or plate glass, commonly used for shop windows and shelves.

Intaglio vitreographs

Intaglio prints are made by abrading, scratching or etching the surface of the glass to produce tiny ink-holding pits. Abrasion is accomplished by grinding with a small high-speed grinder equipped with diamond points, or by sandblasting. The plate may also be etched with glass-etching paste. By these means it is possible to create a variety of marks and textures, from simple lines to tones that resemble ink washes and aquatint. Sandblasting produces consistent tones ranging from delicate tints to solid tone, but those parts of the plate that are not to receive tone must be protected from the onslaught of sand. Contact paper is a very effective resist that produces sharply defined edges. Wet litho ink painted onto the plate resists sandblasting to a greater or lesser extent depending upon the thickness of application. It produces areas

CASE STUDY: DALE CHIHULY

This is a lively example of a print from a glass plate by perhaps the world's most famous glass artist. The approach is reminiscent of Chihuly's drawings and also reflects the bravura of his blown-glass vessels, sculptural pieces and chandeliers.

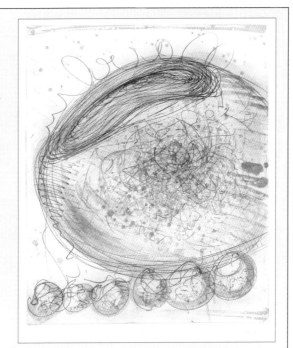

Macchia, Dale Chihuly, USA, 1994. Vitreograph: four-colour intaglio print from glass plates. Limited edition of 50 with 6 artist's proofs. Hand-printed on acid-free BFK Rives white paper. The sheet is 90 x 75 cm and image is 75 x 55 cm. Numbered and signed by the artist. Printed by Judith O'Rourke. Courtesy of Littleton Studios.

of tone with brushy textures and softly defined edges. Glass-etching paste may be applied where filmy or watery tones are desired.

Vitreograph plates processed in the intaglio technique are inked in the same manner as metal intaglio plates. Ink is forced into the pits and grooves in the surface of the plate with a paper or plastic card. Excess ink is removed by wiping the plate with the stiff muslin known to etchers as tarlatan or scrim. Areas of the plate that do not carry imagery are further cleaned with tissue paper. The glass template is printed onto damp paper in an etching press, as one would using a metal etching plate, with the proviso that the glass plate is thicker, and thus the distance between the roller and the press bed must be increased to accommodate it. In printing the vitreograph plate, it is essential that the press bed be level and clean. The glass plate can withstand great pressure when applied uniformly, but it breaks when placed under tension: a lump of dried ink or a piece of grit lodged between the press bed and the plate will cause the glass to crack when pressure is applied. The virtue of this

Judith O'Rourke, Master Printer at Littleton Studios, inking up a glass plate.

rigidity is that, unlike metal, the image-bearing surface of the glass will not deform under repeated runs through the press; therefore, a virtually limitless number of intaglio prints may be pulled without loss of fine detail. Prints in several colours can be made by using multiple plates, each bearing a different element of the whole. Relief prints can also be made by rolling ink onto the surface of a plate that has been worked with intaglio techniques.

Planographic vitreographs

Planographic vitreographs are also known as 'siligraphs'. Like intaglio vitreographs they are printed on an etching press. The ink is applied to the plate with a roller. As in stone or metal-plate lithography, the image areas of the template accept the ink while the non-image areas repel it. To prepare a glass plate for the planographic process it is 'grained' with a muller or small block of glass with 220 Carborundum™ grit and water. The plate is then thoroughly cleaned with water and vinegar. The image is drawn onto the glass with water-soluble materials, such as water-based pencils or crayons, ink, poster paint, etc. To process the plate for printing, silicone caulk (filler) is mixed with turpentine-replacement paint solvent (synthetic turpentine) to a syrup-like consistency. It is applied to the plate using about one teaspoon of the mixture for every 30 cm². The mixture is buffed to a thin layer with a lint-free cloth and allowed to cure for about 12 hours. The silicone mixture adheres to the glass only where it is not blocked by deposits of crayon or ink.

CASE STUDY: STANISLAV LIBENSKY

This is a powerful image by the late eminent artist famed for his cast-glass sculpture, the essence of which is embodied in this image.

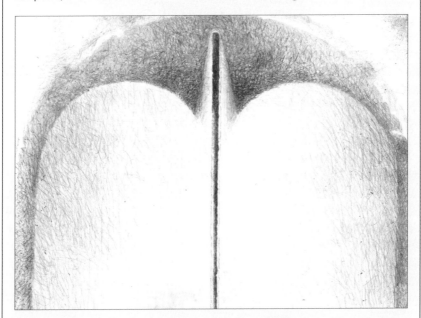

Impress of an Angel, Stanislav Libensky, Czech Republic, 1996. Vitreograph: black and white planographic print from a glass plate. Limited edition of 40 with 2 artist's proofs. Hand-printed on acid-free Arches 88 paper. The sheet is 55 x 65 cm and the image is 31 x 44 cm. Signed and numbered by the artist. Printed by Judith O'Rourke. Courtesy of Littleton Studios.

Gentle washing with warm soapy water removes the drawing materials, leaving open areas of uncoated glass. These are filled with printing ink when the plate is rolled in preparation for printing. The silicone layer resists inking in the areas of the image that are not to be printed. The plate is printed onto damp paper in an etching press. Lighter pressure is required than that necessary to print an intaglio vitreograph.

Advantages of printing from glass

Printing from glass plates presents some challenges but also offers potential advantages for artists. When preparing a plate with an image it is possible to use an original drawing or previous plate as a guide by placing it under the clear-glass plate to be worked upon. Printers who use the intaglio process find that a glass plate is easier to wipe clean than a metal one, allowing for a more striking contrast in the finished print between the open and the printed areas of the image. Some feel that the resistance of glass to wear allows for more consistent large editions. Bright, clean colour is easier to achieve in vitreograph prints, because the relatively inert glass does not discolour the ink through oxidation in the way that metal can. For some artists the challenge and excitement of working from a glass plate as opposed to more conventional metal plates provides an impetus for creativity in itself.

Printing from glass plates onto paper could form the subject for a book in its own right. Therefore, to supplement this brief overview you might wish to consult the following article: 'Vitreography – The art and technique of the glass print', *Printmaking Today*, Vol. 3, No. 3, 1994, p. 25–7. A useful 30-minute video is also available from the Littleton Studios, entitled *Luminous Impressions*.

CONCLUSION

As I have worked on this book it has become increasingly apparent that the methods described in each of the chapters could form books in their own right. A publication of this scale can really only hope to scratch the surface of such large subject areas. Having said that, I hope that it will be of use by indicating the great potential of glass and print for creative expression.

It is important to say that it is creative vision rather than technique that leads to successful artworks. This book cannot provide this vision, but I hope it can indicate some methods by which ideas and creativity might be expressed through glass and print.

Kevin Petrie, University of Sunderland.

GLOSSARY

Acid-etching: the etching of a design into glass using acid.

Annealing: the controlled cooling of glass to even out the temperature throughout the piece in order to reduce the risk of the piece cracking.

Antique glass: flat glass produced by the cylinder method, characterised by air bubbles and streaks. Mainly used in leaded stained-glass work.

Architectural glass: glass used within the context of buildings. Also used to describe stained glass.

Baren: a Japanese instrument used for burnishing the back of paper to produce a relief print. Wooden or metal spoons can be used as an alternative.

Bitumen: (US: 'roofing tar'). A sticky black paint, available from hardware stores. Mainly used in roofing and also as a painted or screenprinted resist for acid-etching glass.

Brunswick Black: a varnish of asphalt or pitch, linseed oil and turpentine, used to give a shiny appearance to metals and other matierals. Can be printed as an acid-etching resist.

Bullseye Glass Co.: a US company based in Portland, Oregon that produces ranges of coloured glass compatible for creative use.

Carborundum: a tradename for silicon carbide, a material used to grind the surface of glass.

Cased glass: blown glass with two different colours combined in layers. One colour forms a skin or case around the other. A layer can be removed by sandblasting or acid-etching to reveal the colour of the other layer.

CMYK: also known as the 'process colours', cyan, magenta, yellow and keyline (black). These colours are printed as halftones and interact together to create 'full colour' images.

Cold colours: term used to describe standard screenprinting colours that can be applied to the surface of glass, and that do not require firing on. Not as durable as fired-on colours.

Copperplate oil: a printing medium made from boiled linseed oil. Used to make inks for etching and engraving.

Cullet: broken or scrap glass introduced to the furnace or kiln for re-melting.

Decal: see Transfer.

Enamels: vitreous pigments coloured with metallic oxides, used for printing, painting and spraying glass and ceramics.

Engraving: in printmaking this refers to the cutting of a design into a metal plate that is inked and printed like an etching plate. In glass, engraving refers to the cutting of a design directly into the surface of glass.

Etching plate: a metal plate, often of copper or zinc, in which a design has been etched by the corrosive action of acid. This creates an intaglio surface into which ink is applied. The inked plate is run through a press with paper under pressure. This imprints the image onto the paper.

Fablon: a trade name for adhesive-backed plastic sheet sometimes known as 'sticky-backed plastic'. Used to make cut stencils that are applied to glass to resist sandblasting.

Firing: the process of fixing paint or enamel onto the surface of glass in a kiln. Also refers to any process of forming glass in a kiln.

Flexography: see photopolymer printing.

Float glass: sheet glass made by floating a continuous ribbon of molten glass into a bath of heated tin. Sometimes known as 'window glass' and characterised by its greenish tinge.

Fusing: the process of melting layers of glass together in a kiln. This is often achieved at around 760°C/1400°F.

Gather: the term used to describe the 'gob' of molten glass that is extracted from the furnace in glass-blowing.

Hot glass: sometimes used to describe glass-blowing. Also used to describe glassmaking techniques whereby objects are created by hand-held tools or by pouring glass into moulds often made of sand.

Intaglio printing: usually refers to printing plates that have the design cut or etched into the flat printing plate, as opposed to a design protruding from the surface of the plate as in relief printing. The intaglio areas of the plates hold the ink while any excess is removed from the surface.

Linisher: (US: wet belt sander). A machine with a belt of abrasive grain or cork for grinding and polishing glass. Often used to remove the sharp edges of glass.

Kiln-formed glass: glass that has been formed, usually into a mould, by the action of heat in a kiln.

Kodatrace: a trade name for a translucent matt drafting film used to prepare positives for printing.

Molochite: calcined china clay used with plaster in the mould mix for kiln-forming glass. Helps to prevent damage to the mould from thermal shock during heating.

Relief printing: sometimes known as block printing. A type of printing where the design is raised in relief. Ink is usually rolled across the surface of this relief. The ink is transferred when brought into contact with the surface to be printed.

Resist: a material that is used to cover glass to mask areas from the action of acid or sandblasting.

Photopolymer printing: an industrial printing technique that uses a flexible relief plate. This process can be used for printing directly onto glass, or plaster moulds can be taken from the relief plates in which glass can be cast. Also known as 'solarplate printing' or flexography.

Planographic: printing processes where the printing plate is flat.

Sandblasting: the use of compressed air to project an abrasive material at the surface of glass in order to create a matt surface or matt designs. Can also create a deeply abraded surface.

Screenprinting: a method of printing where a fine mesh is used, through which ink is pressed with the action of a rubber blade known as a squeegee. Used for the direct application of imagery to the surface of glass or to make transfers.

Silicone: (US: caulk). An adhesive used by glassmakers to join elements together. Also used in vitreography. Silicone rubber is another product used for mould-making.

Silver stain: a type of glass 'paint' which contains silver compounds and produces colours ranging from yellow to deep brown after a firing of around 520-650°C/968-1202°F.

Slumping: a kiln-forming process whereby glass (usually flat glass) is bent in the kiln over or into a former. This can be achieved with plaster, metal or clay moulds or by suspending glass with wires.

Stencil: a mask used to block areas of the mesh in screenprinting and other print methods, to create a design. Also refers to materials applied directly to glass to resist the action of acid or sandblasting. It is often a form of self-adhesive vinyl.

Transfer: also known as **decals**. A printed image (usually screen-printed) on a special transfer or decal paper that can be removed after contact with water and applied to glass and ceramic objects.

Vitreography: a term coined by Harvey Littleton to describe a range of methods for printing onto paper from glass plates.

Vitrify: the process of turning materials into a glass-like form via the action of heat.

DIRECTORY

Glass manufacturers and suppliers

Pilkington
Prescot Road
St Helens WA10 3TT
UK
Tel: +44 (0)1744 692 000
Fax: +44(0)1744 613 049
www.pilkington.co.uk
Float-glass manufacturer.

Bullseye Glass Co.
3610 SE 21 Street
Portland
OR 97202
USA
Tel: +1 503 227 2797
Fax: +1 503 227 3130
sales@bullseyeglass.com
Suppliers of a broad range of compatible glasses.

Pearsons Glass Ltd
Maddrell Street
Liverpool L3 7EH
UK
Tel: +44 (0)151 207 1474
Fax: +44 (0)151 207 2110
pearsons@northwest.co.uk
Suppliers of a broad range of glass including sheet glass and Bullseye.

Glashutte Lamberts
Waldsassen
Schutzenstrasse 1
95652 Waldsassen
Postfach 1106
Germany
Tel: +49 9632 2371
Fax: +49 9632 4880
Manufacturers of antique glass.

English Antique Glass Ltd
Bordesley Hall
Alveschurch
Birmingham B48 7QA
UK
Manufacturers of antique glass.

Transfers, rubber stamps, enamels, printing media, covercoats and transfer papers for glass

Ferro Corporation
1000 Lakeside Avenue
Cleveland
Ohio 44114 7000
USA
Tel: +1 216 641 8080
www.ferro.com
Manufacturers of enamels and printing media for glass and ceramics.

Heraeus GmbH
Produktbereich
Keramische Farben
Postfach 1553
D-6450 Hanau 1
Germany
Manufacturers and suppliers of enamel colours.

Heraeus Materials Limited
Unit A, Cinderhill
Industrial Estate
Weston Coyney Road
Longton
Stoke on Trent
ST3 5LB
UK
Tel: +44 (0)1782 599 423
Fax: +44 (0)1782 599 802

Johnson Matthey Ltd
JM Select
King Street
Fenton
Stoke on Trent ST4 3DF
UK
Tel: +44 (0)1782 339880
jmselect@matthey.com
Enamels, printing media, covercoats and transfers.

K.H. Bailey and Sons Ltd
Marsh Street
Stoke on Trent ST1 5HH
UK
Tel: +44 (0)1782 213811
Fax: +44 (0) 1782 260299
Rubber stamps and open-stock transfers.

Brittains (TR) Ltd
Ivy House Paper Mills
Commercial Road
Hanley
Stoke on Trent ST1 3QS
UK
Tel: +44 (0)1782 202567
Fax: +44 (0) 1782 202157
Manufacturer of transfer/decal papers.

Tullis Russel Coaters
72 North Street
Danbury
Connecticut 06810 8273
USA
Tel: +1 203 778 8721
Fax: +1 203 791 040

GT Paper and Packaging
Hedley Terrace
Lingard Street
Burslem
Stoke on Trent
ST6 2AW
UK

Tel: +44 (0) 1782 577328
Fax: +44 (0) 1782 577068
Suppliers of potter's tissue.

Pamela Morton Ceramics
22b Holt Road
Cromer
Norfolk NR27 9JW
UK
Tel: +44 (0) 1263 512629
*Producer of custom-run
transfers/decals. Will do
relatively short runs.*

Potterycrafts
Campbell Road
Stoke on Trent ST4 4ET
UK
Tel: +44(0)1782 7455000
Fax: +44(0)1782 7466000
www.potterycrafts.co.uk
*Enamels and screenprinting
products.*

John Purcell Paper
15 Rumsey Road
London SW9 0TR
UK
Tel: +44 (0)20 7737 5199
Fax: +44 (0)20 7737 6765
mail@johnpurcell.net
*For paper, True-Grain and
UWET pre-coated transfer
paper.*

General printmaking suppliers

T.N. Lawrence & Son Ltd
208 Portland Road
Hove BN3 5QT, UK
Tel: 0845 644 3232
(+44 [0] 1273 260260)
Fax: 0845 644 3233
(+44 [0] 1273 260270)
artbox@lawrence.co.uk
www.lawrence.co.uk
*For etching, lino and general
printmaking supplies.*

Coates Screen
Cray Avenue
Orpington
Kent BR5 3TT
UK
Tel: +44 (0)1689 899666
*Screens, emulsions and
screenprint machinery.*

Autotype International Ltd
Grove Road
Wantage
Oxon OX12 7BZ
UK
Tel: +44 (0)1235 771111
*Emulsions and films for screen
stencils, for example, 'Autocut'
film and 'TrueGrain'.*

Dan Smith
PO Box 84268
Seattle
WA 98124-5568
www.danielsmith.com

Dick Blick Art Materials
PO Box 1267
Galesburg
Illinois
IL 61402-1267
www.dickblick.com
*General supplies, and small
quantities of enamel.*

Natgraph Ltd
Dabell Avenue
Bleinheim Industrial Estate
Nottingham NG6 8WA
UK
Tel: +44 (0)115 979 5800
info@natgraph.co.uk
www.natgraph.co.uk
Screenprinting equipment.

Sericol Limited
Pysons Road
Broadstairs
Kent CT10 2LE
UK

Tel: +44 (0)1843 866 668
Fax: +44 (0)1843 872 074
Screenprinting products.

Materials for preparing artwork

*Your local art shop will have
basic drawing materials and
drafting films for making
artwork. Typesetters or
Printers Services supply film
positives. For True-Grain see
John Purcell and Autotype
above.*

Ulano Corp.
110 Third Ave
Brooklyn
NY 11217
USA
Fax: +1 718 802 1119
*Suppliers of Amberlith,
Rubylith, and coating emulsion.*

Folex Limited
18/19 Monkspath Business
Park
Shirley
Solihull
West Midlands B90 4NY
UK
Tel: +44 (0) 121 733 3833
Fax: +44 (0) 121 733 3222
sales@folex.co.uk
www.folex.co.uk
*Suppliers of laser film
(matt/clear).*

Folex Imaging
24 Just Road
Fairfield
NJ 07004
USA
Tel: +1 201 575 4500
Fax: +1 201 575 4646
www.folex-usa.com

Photopolymer/ flexography plates

Toyobo Co. Ltd Graphic
Arts Department
2–8 Dojima Hama 2
Chome
Kita-ku
Osaka 530-8230
Japan
Tel: + 81-6-6348-3058
Fax: + 81-6-6348-3099
www.toyobo.co.jp/e/seihin/
xk/print/
*Manufacturers and suppliers
of photopolymer plates.*

Nicoll Graphics
at Openshaw International
Woodhouse Road
Todmorden
Lancashire OL14 5TP
UK
Tel: +44 (0) 1706 811 413

Resists for sandblasting

AICELLO Chemical Europe
GmbH
Xantener Strasse 1
Mulheim a.d. Ruhr
Germany
Tel: +49(0) 208/30 69 15 10
Fax: +49(0) 208/30 69 15 11
www.aicello-photomask.com
*Suppliers of APM films. For
the UK, if you contact
AICELLO Chemical they will
give you the contact details of
your nearest UK supplier.*

CSH Cabanes SL
C/ Abogado Andrs
Charques No 3
Alicante 03006
Spain
Tel: +34 965 28 15 20
Fax: +34 965 28 43 81
cabanes@cshcabanes.e.tele

fonica.net.
Suppliers of Rayzist film.

Vitro Mask Ltd
Dundas House
214a Conkwell
Bradford on Avon
BA15 2FJ
Tel: +44 (0)1225 722 315
Fax: +44 (0)1225 722 318
*Suppliers of SBX liquid
emulsion and APM films.*

The Glass Scribe
Spencer House
Caberfeidh Ave
Digwell IV15 9TD
UK
Tel: +44 (0)1349 867 088
Fax: +44 (0)1349 867 089
*The Glass Scribe supplies
sample packs showing the
various stages of the process
including sheets of vellum.*

T-Fix Extra Spay supplied
by Sericol Ltd
*For local supplier contact:
Sericol Ltd (see above)
Adhesives: the manufacturer
supplies its own adhesives in
the form of a sandblastproof
tape.*

Crystal Galleries Ltd
38–42 Westbourne Grove
North Ormesby
Middlesbrough
Cleveland
TS3 6EF
UK
Tel: +44 (0)1642 225 799
Fax: +44 (0)1642 217 928
www.crystalgalleries.co.uk.
*Supplier of Ryazist
photomasks.*

PhotoBrasive Systems
4832 Grand Avenue

Duluth
MN 55807
USA
Tel: +1 (218) 628-2002
Fax: +1 (218) 628-2064
www.photobrasive.com
*Main US supplier of SBX
liquid emulsion, APM films
and the DuPont -
manufactured RapidMask.*

Rayzist Photomask, Inc.
955 Park Center Drive
Vista
CA 92081 8312
USA
Tel: 800 729 9478
Direct Tel: +1 760 727
8185
Fax: +1 760 727 2986
www.rayzist.com.
Main Rayzist supplier.

Etching resists and pastes

ImagOn™ ULTRA
Intaglio Printmakers
62 Southwark Bridge Road
London SE1 0AS
UK
Tel: +44 (0)20 7928 2633
Fax: +44 (0)20 7928 2711
www.intaglioprintmakers.
com

PHOTEC
Edinburgh Printmakers
23 Union Street
Edinburgh EH1 3LR
UK
Tel: +44 (0)131 5572479

Sally Dyas
Rocquette Villa
Rocquette Lane
St Peter Port
Guernsey GY1 1XT, UK
www.sdyas.demon.co.uk

ImagOn ULTRA
Parker Sydney Fine Art
Suppliers
3 Cambridge Street
The Rocks
Sydney 2000, NSW
Australia
Tel: +61 (02) 9247 9979

Praga Industries Co. Ltd
38 Thatcher Avenue
Scarborough
Ontario
Canada M1M 2M2
Tel: +1 800 844 9421
Tel: +1 416 281 0511
Fax: +1 416 281 0056
www.praga.com

Mico Printing Supplies Ltd
Contact Mrs J. Batt
+44 (0)20 7354 1431
www.micochem.co.uk
*Glass-etching products,
including screenprinting
pastes and general
screenprint products.*

Photography and glass

Rockland Colloid Corp.
Box 376
Piermont
NY 10968
USA
Tel: +1 845 359 5559
Fax: +1 845 365 6663
*Supplier of Liquid Light,
Liquid Light VC (variable
contrast) and AG Plus (a
higher-speed emulsion).*

Jessops
Jessop House
Scudamore Road
Leicester LE3 1TZ
UK
Tel: +44 (0)116 232 6000
Supplier of Liquid Light and a

*wide range of darkroom
chemistry for printing and
processing.*

Silverprint Ltd
12 Valentine Place
London SE1 8QH
Tel: +44 (0)207 620 0844
www.silverprint.co.uk
*Supplier of Liquid Light and a
wide range of darkroom
chemistry for printing and
processing.*

Digital prints and wet-release laser films

Cuccolini NTD (UK) Ltd
14 High St
Tunstall
Stoke on Trent ST6 5TF
UK
Tel: +44 (0)1782 818111
Fax: +44 (0)1782 817755
sales.cuccolini@virgin.net
*Suppliers of digital-transfer
printers and toners.*

Polycarta Limited
Unit A, Slippery Lane
Hanley
Stoke on Trent ST1 4JA
UK
Tel: +44 (0)1782 210650
Fax: +44 (0)1782 286676
info@polycarta.co.uk
Suppliers of digital transfers.

Digital Ceramics Systems
Taylor Buildings
Clough St
Hanley
Stoke on Trent ST1 4BA
UK
Tel: +44 (0)1782 215400
Fax: +44 (0)1782 263000
info@digitalceramics.com
www.digitalceramics.com
Suppliers of digital transfers.

Design Point Decal, Inc.
10 Midland Ave
Port Chester
NY 10580
USA
Tel: +1 (914) 935 3300
Fax +1 (914) 935 3310
info@designpoint.com
www.designpoint.com

Dennis Caffrey
Urban Clay Inc.
2424 E. 55th St
Los Angeles
CA 90058
USA
Tel: +1 (323) 581 8702
Fax: +1 (323) 581 0198
www.urbanclay.com

Lazertran Ltd
8 Alban Square
Aberaeron
Ceredigion SA46 0AD
Wales, UK
Tel: +44 (0)1545 571149
Fax: +44 (0)1545 571187
mic@lazertran.com
www.lazertran.com/order.
htm
Lazertran (laser-printed wet-release decal paper).

Glass and print studios/fabricators

Derix Glass Studios
D-65232 Taunusstein
Platterstraße 94
Germany
Tel: +49 06128 96680
studio@derix.com
www.derix.com

Franz Mayer of Munich, Inc.
(Mayer'sche
Hofkunstanstalt GmbH)
Seidlstrasse 25
80335 Munich

Germany
Tel: +49 089 54 59 62 0
info@mayer-of-munich.com
www.mayer-of-munich.com

Littleton Studios
232 Eastridge Drive
Spruce Pine
NC 28777-6341
USA
glassman@vol.com
Vitreography.

Proto Studios Ltd
Units 13–15
Salisbury Road Business
Park
Salisbury Road
Pewsey
Wiltshire SN9 5PZ
Tel: +44 (0)1672 563322
Fax: +44 (0)1672 564866
info@protostudios.com

A selection of academic institutions offering glass courses

Edinburgh College of Art
Lauriston Place
Edinburgh
Tel: +44 (0)131 229 9311
www.eca.ac.uk

University of the Arts,
London
Central St Martins
Southampton Row
London WC1B 4AP
Tel: +44 (0)20 7514 7000

Royal College of Art
Ceramics and Glass
Kensington Gore
London SW7 2EU
Tel: +44 (0)20 7590 4444
www.rca.ac.uk

Swansea Institute of
Higher Education
Mount Pleasant
Swansea SA1 6ED
Wales, UK
Tel: +44 (0)1792 481 000
enquiry@sihe.ac.uk
www.sihe.co.uk

University of Sunderland
National Glass Centre
Liberty Way
Sunderland,
Tyne and Wear
Tel: +44(0)191 515 2000
www.sunderland.ac.uk

Wolverhampton University
Glass Dept
Molineux Street
Wolverhampton WV1 1SB
Tel: +44 (0)191 515 2000
www.wlv.ac.uk

Canberra School of Art
The ANU School of Art
GPO Box 804
Canberra
ACT 2601 Australia
csa.reception@anu.edu.au
www.anu.edu.au

Monash University
Caulfield Campus
900 Dandenong Rd
Caulfield East (Melbourne)
Victoria 3145, Australia
www.monash.edu.au

Sydney College of the Arts
University of Sydney
15 Rozelle
2039 NSW Australia
Tel: +61 2 9351 4079
info@usyd.edu.au
www.usyd.edu.au

Pilchuck Glass School
107 South Main Street
Seattle
WA 98104 USA
www.pilchuck.com

Staatliche Glasfachschule
Rheinbach
Zentrum fur Glass-
Keramik-Grafik
Zu den Fichten 19
D53359 Rheinbach
Germany
Tel: +49 2226 4425

Journals
Printmaking Today
Cello Press Limited
Office G18, Spinners Court
55 West End
Witney
Oxon OX28 1NH
Tel: + 44 (0) 1993 701002
cellomail@pt.cellopress.co.uk
www.printmakingtoday.com

Neus Glas
Veragsgesellschaft
Ritterbach GmbH
PO Box 1820
D-50208 Frechen
Germany

Websites

www.gatewaytoglass.org
Educational resource for glass. Artist database, exhibitions, journal, education and research.

www.corning.com
Glass technology-led products.

www.printmaker.co.uk
Useful listing of printmaking suppliers and related sites worldwide.

BIBLIOGRAPHY AND FURTHER READING

Benton, E., 'John Brooks in Birmingham', E.C.C. Transactions, vol. 6, p 3, 1970, p.162.

Blakeslee, A.L., 'Printing Photos inside Glass' in *Popular Science*, Nov. 1947.

Bray, C., *Dictionary of Glass – Materials and Techniques*, A&C Black, 2001.

Byrd, J.F., 'Littreography' in *Glass: The Urban Glass Quarterly*, no. 72, Fall 1998, pp. 12–25.

Charleston, R.J., *Decoration of Glass – Part 4:* The Glass Circle, 1972.

Cummings, K., *Techniques of Kiln-Formed Glass*, A&C Black.

Freeman, P., 'Lithographic and Screenprinted Transfers' in *Ceramic Industries Journal*, no. 92, December 1983, pp. 24–7.

Garbowski, B.J., *Photosensitive Glass – Trail of Research*, Rakow Research Library, Corning Glass Works, 1978.

Hajdamach, Charles R., *British Glass 1800–1914*, Antique Collectors Club, 1991.

Harrison, M., 'Combining mediums – Brian Clarke and Linda McCartney', Brian Clarke and Linda McCartney – Collaborations, Le Musée Suisse du Vitrail, Romont, 1997.

Hoskins, S., *Water-based Screenprinting*, A&C Black, 2001.

Houk, P., 'Glass and the Photographic Sensitivity: A random sampling of artists and processes.' The Glass Art Society Journal, GAS, Seattle, WA 2004, pp.36-39.

Kessler, J., *Luminous Impressions – Prints from Glass Plates*, North Carolina: Mint Museum 1987, p. 11.

Kerslake, K. A.,'Vitreography – The art and technique of the glass print' in *Printmaking Today*, vol. 3, no. 3, 1994, pp. 25–7.

Littleton Studios, *Luminous Impressions* (video), ©1997, Grasberg/Littleton Productions.

Longley, D., *Printmaking with Photopolymer Plates*, Illumination Press, 1998.

Mara, T., *The Thames and Hudson Manual of Screen Printing*, Thames and Hudson, 1976.

Papadopoulos, G., *Glass Handbook: Lamination*, A&C Black, 2004.

Petrie, K., 'Integrated Glass Prints' in the 'Research Projects' section of 'Learning about Glass' on the Gateway to Glass website, www.gatewaytoglass.org, 2004.

Rothenstein, M., *Linocuts & Woodcuts*, Studio Books, 1962.

Scott, P., Ceramics and Print, A&C Black, 2002

Semenoff, N., 'Waterless Lithography I, II & III', *Printmaking Today*, vol. 4, nos. 1, 2 & 3, 1995. (The processes described can be applied to glass.)

Stookey, S.D., 'Photosensitive Glass – A new photographic medium', reprinted from *Industrial and Engineering Chemistry*, vol. 41, p. 856, April 1949.

Turner, S., *Screen Printing Techniques*, B.T. Batsford, 1976.

Watney, B. and Charleston, R.J., 'Petitions for Patents concerning Porcelain, Glass and Enamels with special reference to Birmingham, "The Great Toyshop of Europe"' in *English Ceramic Circle*, 1966, vol. 6, no. 2, pp. 57–123.

Westley, A., *Relief Printing*, A&C Black, 2001.

Whale, G. and Barfield, N., *Digital Printmaking*, A&C Black, 2001.

Williams-Wood, C., *English Transfer-Printed Pottery and Porcelain*, London: Faber and Faber, 1981.

INDEX